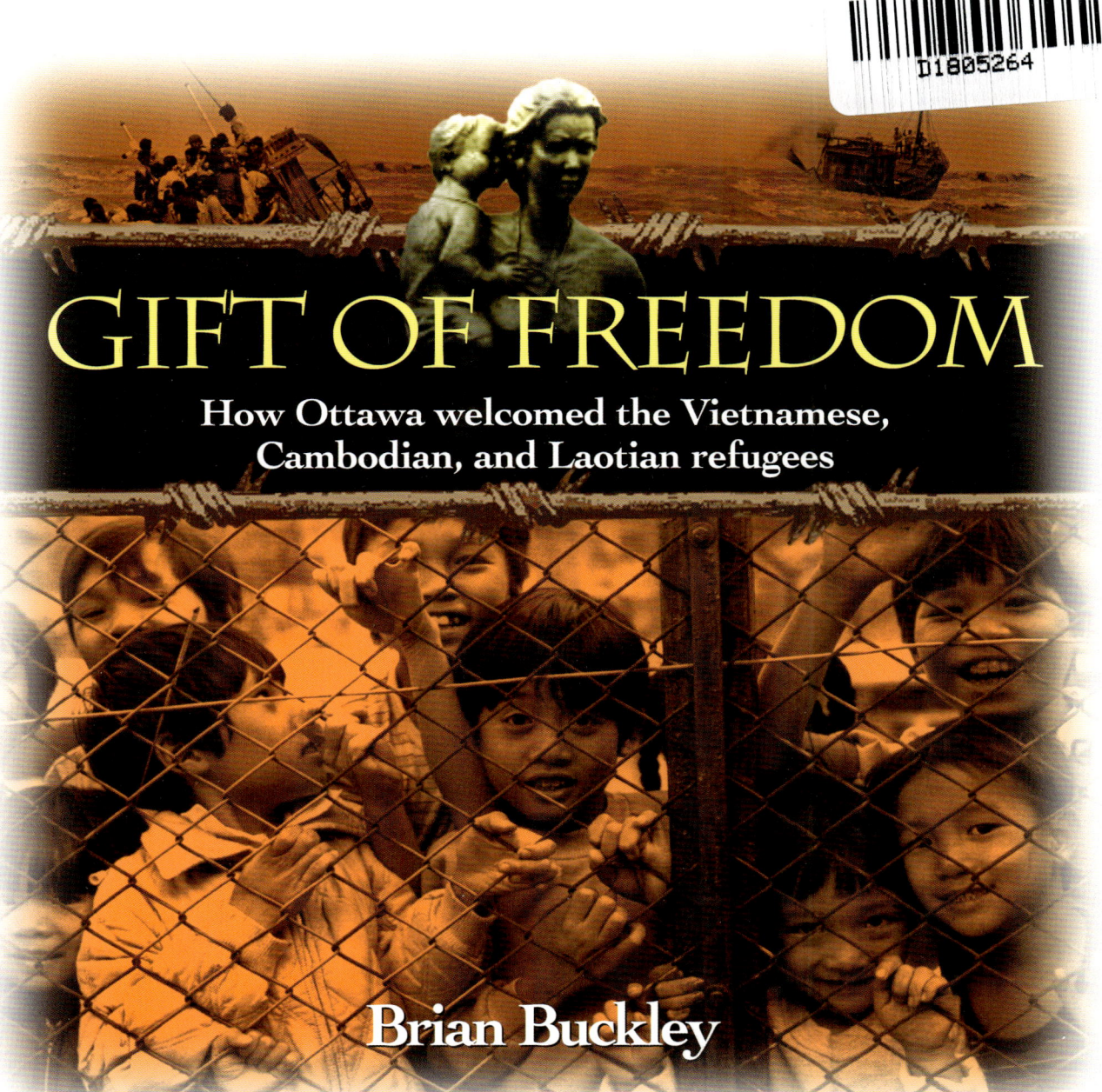

GIFT OF FREEDOM

How Ottawa welcomed the Vietnamese, Cambodian, and Laotian refugees

Brian Buckley

Published by

 **GENERAL STORE PUBLISHING HOUSE**

499 O'Brien Road, Box 415
Renfrew, Ontario, Canada K7V 4A6
Telephone (613) 432-7697 or 1-800-465-6072

ISBN 978-1-897113-91-2
Printed and bound in Canada

Cover design by: Lê-Phan
Formatting and printing by Custom Printers of Renfrew Ltd.

No part of this book may be reproduced, stored in a retrieval system or transmitted in any form or by any means, without the prior written permission of the publisher or, in case of photocopying or other reprographic copying, a licence from Access Copyright (Canadian Copyright Licensing Agency), 1 Yonge Street, Suite 1900, Toronto, Ontario, M5C 1E6.

Library and Archives Canada Cataloguing in Publication

Buckley, Brian
    Gift of freedom / Brian Buckley.

ISBN 978-1-897113-91-2

    1. Refugees--Vietnam. 2. Refugees--Cambodia. 3. Refugees--Laos. 4. Refugees--Ontario--Ottawa--History--20th century. 5. Refugees--Services for--Ontario--Ottawa--History--20th century. 6. Southeast Asians--Ontario--Ottawa--Social conditions--20th century. 7. Vietnam War, 1961-1975--Refugees. I. Title.

HV640.5.V5B83 2008   362.87'089959071   C2007-906969-X

GIFT OF FREEDOM:

How Ottawa welcomed the Vietnamese, Cambodian and Laotion Refugees

Brian Buckley

Courtesy of the University of Texas Libraries, The University of Texas at Austin.

ACKNOWLEDGEMENTS

In the world of the theatre "angels" are those who provide tangible support and encouragement for a work. This work has been sustained by many angels.

The book was funded by grants from the Community Foundation of Ottawa and the Heritage Funding Program of the City of Ottawa. I wish to express my appreciation to both organizations for their timely and valuable support. The Vietnamese Canadian Centre deserves my special thanks. The Centre was consistently generous and helpful in giving me access to a wide variety of materials, in locating persons and resources important to the story, and in providing office space and support for meetings.

The present work owes a great deal to the members of the Project 4000 Book Committee:

Barbara Gamble, with the eye of an artist - and the mind of a senior executive;

Doctor Can Le, with broad and deep knowledge of the refugee experience in Ottawa - and a matchless ability to identify relevant sources and leads;

Sue Pike, with her own extensive experience as a writer and editor - and intuitive sense of what the work required;

Eleanor Ryan, the "keeper of the flame" - and conserver of a unique collection of primary materials.

Collectively and individually the Committee members were an unfailing source of practical support and constructive advice.

The text benefited as well from the contributions of three outside readers, each of whom brought a unique set of credentials to the project: Marion Dewar, Ottawa's fifty-second Mayor, who initiated Project 4000; Russ Mills, former editor of the Ottawa Citizen, who witnessed the events from a uniquely well placed vantage point; and Ngoc Tran, a former refugee with first-hand experience of the challenges of rebuilding a life in a new country. The reviewers examined each chapter as it was drafted and provided consistently thoughtful comment and encouragement.

The work could not have gone forward had it not been for the willingness of those whose lives were touched by Project 4000 – former refugees, sponsors, volunteers – to share their memories and experiences. Some three dozen people relived the era with me, providing first-hand accounts of the trials and the triumphs of what many consider Ottawa's finest moment. Although some stories had their tragic elements, far stronger were the themes of courage and compassion that emerged time and again from the highly personal accounts of the participants.

I am indebted as well to my editor, Laura Byrne Paquet for her intelligent and perceptive treatment of the manuscript. "I think of it as it should have been, with its prolixities docked, its dullnesses enlivened, its fads eliminated, its truths multiplied" wrote H.W.Fowler in introducing his <u>Modern English Usage.</u> If the published text approaches Fowler's vision in any respect, it is very much thanks to Laura's excellent work.

Many other angels contributed along the way. I particularly wish to thank Clementine-Ann Remedios and Gisèle Nyembwe of the Ottawa office of the United Nations High Commissioner for Refugees (UNHCR), Liisa Tuominen, librarian at the Ottawa Citizen, Hariette Fried of the City of Ottawa Archives, and the helpful and effective personnel of Library and Archives Canada and the Ottawa Public Library. I also want to express my appreciation to Tim Gordon and his colleagues at General Store Publishing House for making the production and publication of this volume a positive and pleasant experience.

Lê-Phan, a gifted graphic artist and photographer, gave generously of his time and talent to design the covers and contributed several of the pictures reproduced in the text. The front cover images appear with the permission of UNHCR and Pham The Trung, creator of the Vietnamese Commemorative Monument, Refugee Mother and Child inaugurated by the Vietnamese Canadian Federation in Ottawa on April 30, 1995. The back cover images appear courtesy of Phuong Nguyen, Diep Trinh, and Lê-Phan.

Whatever merits the book possesses should properly be attributed to others. Its weaknesses and errors however are entirely my own. Although a great many people contributed to the work I exercised full editorial control over its contents. Accordingly, the bouquets should be addressed to those mentioned above, and the brickbats to me.

A PRAYER FOR LAND

Lost in the tempests

Out on the open seas

Our small boats drift.

We seek for land

During endless days and endless nights.

We are the foam

Floating on the vast ocean.

We are the dust

Wandering in endless space.

Our cries are lost in the howling wind.

Without food, without water

Our children lie exhausted

Until they cry no more.

We thirst for land

But are turned back from every shore.

Our distress signals rise and rise again

But the passing ships do not stop.

How many boats have perished?

How many families lie beneath the waves?

Lord Jesus, do you hear the prayer of our flesh?

Lord Buddha, do you hear our voice

From the abyss of death?

O solid shore,

We long for you!

We pray for mankind to be present today!

We pray for land to stretch out its arms to us!

We pray that hope be given us

Today, from any land.

Unknown Vietnamese poet, 1978

PROLOGUE

An Song Hoang sits on the patio of his home in Ottawa's Centretown, pouring green tea for his visitor. The snug clapboard house is trim and lovingly maintained. It is a bright autumn day and the mellow old patio bricks radiate a memory of summer. Flowering plants abound, and nestling in the corner is a two-level structure for growing children to use—and even sleep in during the long, warm summer nights.

An, now nearly 60, is describing the events that led him to flee his native Vietnam almost 30 years earlier. After several months in a Thai refugee camp, he learned that Canada had agreed to accept him as a refugee. He was so moved, he recalls, that he composed a song to express his gratitude. After a little prompting, he sings it, *a cappella*, for his visitor.

The conversation turns to children and family. An cannot keep his paternal pride from showing as he recounts how well his two young daughters are doing in school. As the interview moves toward its conclusion, An takes out a few photos and newspaper clippings and sets them on the patio table. One picture in particular, a dramatic image of the South China Sea, clearly summons up harrowing memories. "You know," he says, looking at the roiling waters, "I don't know how we ever found the courage to do what we did." His face then breaks into a wide grin as he adds, "But I'm very glad that we did."

The courage displayed by An and millions like him who refused to surrender to a hostile fate, and the compassion shown by the citizens of Ottawa in creating Project 4000 to welcome strangers into their lives, are the interwoven themes of this book.

CONTENTS

ACKNOWLEDGEMENTS v

A PRAYER FOR LAND vii

PROLOGUE viii

CHAPTER 1: CANADA AND THE 1
SOUTHEAST ASIAN REFUGEES
A Note by the Honourable Flora MacDonald .. 1

CHAPTER 2: PORTRAIT OF A CRISIS ... 5
Conflict and Upheaval in Southeast Asia 5
Refugee Movements After the Vietnam War .. 7
Regional Responses 11
The *Hai Hong* Affair 15
The Refugees and the World 19

CHAPTER 3: PROJECT 4000: ORIGINS . 27
The Canadian Context 27
Mayor Marion Dewar 30
First Steps 34
The Lansdowne Park Rally 36
Structure and Resources 41

CHAPTER 4: PROJECT 4000: 47
IMPLEMENTATION
West Meets East: First Impressions 47
Organizational Developments 51
Loss and Recovery 53
Evolution of a Mandate 59
Rebuilding Lives 61
Phasing Out 63
Milestones 65
Looking Back 69
Results 70

CHAPTER 5: EPILOGUE **73**
Points of Reference **73**
Steps on a Journey **75**
The 25th Anniversary Celebrations **78**
Passing the Torch **81**

CHÀO CANADA **84**

CHAPTER NOTES **87**

BIBLIOGRAPHY **92**

INDEX **96**

ABOUT THE AUTHOR **97**

CHAPTER 1

CANADA AND THE SOUTHEAST ASIAN REFUGEES

A Note by the Honourable Flora MacDonald

I am delighted that the full story of Project 4000 is finally being told. As Canadians, we sometimes seem more inclined to focus on our failings than to celebrate our successes. Project 4000, and the larger story of our efforts to assist the Southeast Asian refugees of which it forms an integral part, were both successes in the fullest sense of the word. They deserve to be remembered as important and positive chapters in our national story.

The exodus of refugees from Vietnam, Cambodia and Laos that began in the aftermath of the Vietnam War and continued for two decades was one of the largest humanitarian emergencies of the second half of the 20th century. It may well have been the most complex. Between 1975 and 1995, more than 3 million people left their homelands to seek shelter wherever they could find it. Of this number, 2 million were eventually resettled far beyond the region, primarily in North America, Western Europe and Australia.

The acute phase of the long-running emergency that the world came to know as the "Boat People Crisis" began in late 1978 and continued until the end of 1980. The flows of refugees from the three countries became a flood, as people fled by any and every means. Hundreds of thousands died; victims of nature and—too often—their fellow human beings. The scale of suffering was appalling. The needs were so great that the neighbouring countries in which the exiles first sought refuge feared for their own survival.

On June 4, 1979, I was sworn in as Secretary of State for External Affairs (Foreign Minister) in the government led by the Right Honourable Joe Clark. Within weeks, Mr. Clark and I were on our way to attend a Group of Seven Summit in

Tokyo, where much of the discussion among foreign ministers focused on the spreading Southeast Asian humanitarian emergency. Events moved quickly. With desperation growing throughout the region, the United Nations organized a conference to address the crisis to begin in Geneva on July 20, 1979.

In preparing for that event, I was able to persuade Mr. Clark and my Cabinet colleagues that Canada should show leadership by radically increasing the number of refugees we were prepared to resettle from 8,000 to 50,000. Two days before I left for Geneva, we announced that Canada was prepared to accept up to 50,000 Southeast Asian refugees by the end of 1980 (a target later increased to 60,000). While I do not want to make any excessive claims, I think it is fair to say that our initiative played an important part in encouraging other countries of permanent resettlement to step forward. Certainly the Geneva conference was far more successful than many had predicted, marking an important milestone on the road to developing a coherent, multilateral, long-term approach to the crisis.

The response of the Canadian people was nothing short of magnificent. People across the country had been deeply affected by the sufferings of the refugees and were anxious to help. While some opposition existed, the most articulate, energetic and persuasive voices were those who wanted Canada to act immediately. Large segments of Canadian public opinion were already well ahead of us, primed and ready for action. Our national response was such that by the end of 1980, Canada had taken in a proportionately higher number of refugees than any other Western country of permanent resettlement. The vigour and generosity of our actions were such that in 1986, the Office of the United Nations High Commissioner for Refugees (UNHCR) awarded its Nansen Medal to the people of Canada, the only time that an entire people has been so honoured.

Nowhere was the Canadian response stronger or more effective than in Ottawa and the surrounding capital region. In June 1979, Mayor Marion Dewar called upon her fellow citizens to help relieve the plight of the refugees and launched Project 4000 to provide a practical means for them to do so. Inspired by her personal example and the vision she articulated, the people of the capital region responded with a massive display of generosity and support. Within days, Project 4000—a program to resettle up to 4,000 Southeast Asian refugees permanently in Ottawa—was up and running. Moreover, its impact was felt far beyond the confines of the region. Marion challenged the mayors of other Canadian cities to follow Ottawa's example. Many did, thereby extending and strengthening our national response.

Project 4000 proved influential in other ways as well. As it gathered momentum, no federal political figure or official working in the capital could remain unaware of the extent of local popular support for prompt and effective action to assist the refugees. Project 4000 demonstrated beyond any possible doubt the strength of grassroots support for action, thereby easing the task of those of us at the federal level arguing for a radically higher national resettlement target.

Almost three decades have passed since those event-filled days. Looking back, it is clear to me that Project 4000, and the broader national response, were total and unqualified successes. I have long been convinced that Canada does well by doing good, and the role we played in dealing with the refugee crisis demonstrates the point very effectively. Ottawa, like Canada, gained large numbers of new citizens who quickly became self-supporting and contributed directly to our economic growth. It has been deeply gratifying over the years to witness how the former refugees and their children, through perseverance and hard work, have moved steadily to assume their rightful place in mainstream Canadian society. Our cultural resources have grown and diversified, to our lasting gain. Perhaps most importantly, ordinary Canadians learned that when they summon up the best within them in pursuit of a generous cause, the results are nothing short of amazing.

It has been my great good fortune to have participated in the public life of my country for many years. Nothing in my long career gives me deeper satisfaction than the role I was privileged to play in our response to the Southeast Asian refugee crisis. That the story of Project 4000—an encounter of courage and compassion—is now being told adds greatly to that satisfaction.

CHAPTER 2

PORTRAIT OF A CRISIS

*When sorrows come, they come not single spies,
But in battalions.*

—*Hamlet*, Act IV, Scene V

Conflict and Upheaval in Southeast Asia

No strangers to turmoil throughout their long history, the peoples of Vietnam, Cambodia and Laos entered a particularly turbulent era in the mid-19th century. France's efforts to establish a colonial empire in the region by force of arms, though temporarily successful, soon gave rise to an indigenous opposition. Although the French were able to maintain control of what was then referred to as "French Indochina," the cost of doing so—to the inhabitants of the region and to themselves—rose steadily over the decades. Japan's seizure of the region in 1940, with the acquiescence of the French Vichy regime, brought no respite. The peoples of the area, particularly the Vietnamese, soon came to regard the Japanese as simply another in the long list of foreign invaders they had known and responded with guerrilla war.

In the aftermath of World War II, France's attempt to re-establish control over its former colonies and the local opposition it engendered quickly resulted in renewed violence. The anti-French forces, though often nationalist in inspiration, gradually coalesced around the Vietnamese communists, led by Ho Chi Minh.

Fighting escalated into full-scale war in 1946 and continued for eight years until the French, following their defeat at Dien Bien Phu, acknowledged that they had lost what has come to be known as the first Indochina war. Although the Geneva Agreement of 1954 formally ended the conflict, it brought no lasting peace. Vietnam was partitioned into two political entities (pending elections that were never held). The stage was set for the continuation of a complex politico-military conflict between Hanoi and Saigon, the respective capitals of a firmly communist Democratic Republic of Vietnam (DRV) and a staunchly anti-communist Republic of Vietnam (RVN). That over a million northerners fled south following the establishment of a communist government in Hanoi, while 130,000 pro-communist elements fled north, reinforced the political orientations of both states. Each government in turn obtained—or had thrust upon it—significant military and political support from external powers. North Vietnam received extensive assistance from the then-Communist Bloc, notably the Soviet Union and China, while South Vietnam relied on the United States and several of its regional allies. Hanoi also developed significant popular support among southerners who interpreted the conflict predominantly as an anti-colonial struggle directed toward national reunification. Over the two decades that it harrowed the region, the Vietnam conflict was, at once, a proxy war between East and West, a struggle between contending ideologies, an interstate conflict among local powers, and a guerrilla war.

Although Washington had initially looked askance at France's attempt to re-impose itself in the region, the onset of the Cold War—particularly North Korea's invasion of South Korea in 1950—persuaded American policy-makers that they had little choice but to support Paris. The "domino theory" was then much in vogue, holding that unless the communists were actively opposed, the non-communist states of Asia and the Pacific would fall, one by one, to aggressive communist expansionism. Despite its lack of a direct military role in the first Indochina war, the United States became an increasingly important source of material, economic and political support for the French as that conflict unfolded.

With the defeat of the French, the United States was drawn into—or sought out—steadily greater levels of direct involvement in the ongoing politico-military struggle between North and South Vietnam. From a handful of military advisors sent in 1950 to screen French requests for assistance, the American military presence grew to 16,000 by 1964 and over half a million by 1969. Hanoi, in turn, steadily raised its military commitment, tightened its control over the southern insurgents who had borne the brunt of the fighting, and drew upon ever-greater levels of support from the Soviet Union and China. The hostilities not only intensified between the main belligerents but also spread beyond them. In due course, Cambodia and Laos were drawn into the maelstrom.

Despite the very large American military role, by the late 1960s an increasing number of Americans—particularly after the communist Tet Offensive of 1968—came to conclude that the war could not be won. The newly elected Nixon administration began to seek ways to extricate the U.S. A policy of "Vietnamization" was adopted, in which negotiations were to be pursued with the North Vietnamese while simultaneous efforts were made to build up South Vietnam's military capacity. Following the conclusion of the Paris Peace Accords in January 1973, the U.S. accelerated the withdrawal of its combat troops from Vietnam. Although the South Vietnamese fought on alone for another two years, the strategic balance had shifted decisively in favour of Hanoi. On April 30 1975, Saigon fell and the victorious communist forces gained full control of the South.

Obscured by this brief historical summary is an immense record of death and destruction, suffering and loss. The Vietnam War alone is thought to have cost the lives of between 2 million and 5.4 million people, the majority of them civilians.[1] Many more were injured or maimed. The physical and cultural legacies of generations were destroyed and traditional ways of life fractured, sometimes beyond repair. Massive American use of chemical defoliants between 1961 and 1971 inflicted damage on humans, animals and plant life that persists to this day. One of the darkest chapters of human depravity in the 20th century was written in Cambodia, where the genocidal Pol Pot regime massacred an estimated 2.4 million of its own people, a third of Cambodia's population.[2] Nor was the suffering limited to these groups. The protracted hostilities regularly resulted in large numbers of people being uprooted from their homes, dispossessed of their goods, and severed from their communities and cultures.

People become refugees for many reasons. In some cases, flight is the only response possible to a threat that is direct and immediate; in others, a dangerous and uncertain exile gradually becomes preferable to an intolerable situation that promises only to deteriorate. The decision to leave is almost always an agonizing one, a tenuous victory of hope over despair. For those who decide to leave, flight means losing not only their possessions and places in the society that has nurtured them from birth, but also, often, their most cherished relationships, culture, language and the "mental map" that has allowed them to make sense of the world. Equally clear is that great courage and determination are required. To depart into exile is to refuse defeat at the hands of a hostile fate; to hazard all—life, family, possessions, future—on a single, final act of defiance.

REFUGEE MOVEMENTS AFTER THE VIETNAM WAR

Southeast Asia's unremitting conflict, as noted earlier, regularly resulted in the large-scale uprooting and displacement of populations. At the height of the Vietnam War in the late 1960s, an estimated 10 million people in South Vietnam—half of the population—had been displaced within their own borders.[3] The "boat people" who would impose themselves on the conscience of the world in 1978–79 were the most dramatic, but not the only, act in a complex human tragedy that had begun years earlier and would continue for decades.

In the final days before the fall of Saigon in April 1975, many Vietnamese linked to the South Vietnamese government or to the Americans fled the country. Some 140,000 were evacuated with the departing American forces and resettled in the United States. At least 12,000 more fled by sea to neighbouring non-communist countries.[4] Although the flow slowed to a trickle by the end of 1975, small-scale departures continued for some time.

The communist victory caused enormous anxiety throughout South Vietnam, and not only among those who had actively supported the former government. Nonetheless, a great many people adopted a "wait and see" attitude, hoping to find some way to accommodate themselves to their new political realities. They were soon to conclude that they had no future under the new regime.

The victorious communists methodically set about imposing their will throughout Vietnamese territory. Compulsory political "re-education" was decreed for members of the defeated armed forces and administration. All facets of South Vietnam as a political entity were expunged; the provisional revolutionary government established in the South immediately after victory was dissolved, and in July 1976 North and South were unified as the Socialist Republic of Vietnam. Saigon was renamed Ho Chi Minh City and the free market economy of the South was progressively subordinated to central planning from the North. A number of "new economic zones" were established, often in remote undeveloped parts of the country, to which many southerners were forcibly relocated.

These policies directly affected substantial numbers of people. Over a million Vietnamese were sent to the re-education camps, tens of thousands of whom were imprisoned until the late 1980s.[5] As for the new economic zones, one contemporary source estimated that one and a half million people were forcibly relocated to them,[6] often city dwellers with little in the way of the experience, skills or resources needed to live in primitive agricultural communities.

Faced with international accusations of large-scale human rights abuses the new regime defended its political re-education camps and new economic zones as necessary to deal with the security threat posed by its former adversaries and the country's massive post-war reconstruction needs. In many cases, however, individuals were interned without formal charge or trial. Moreover, conditions were undeniably harsh, particularly in the re-education camps.

Scanty food rations, hard labour, lack of medical care and brutal disciplinary measures all contributed to the deaths of tens of thousands of prisoners. Whatever the formal rationale for the programs, those subjected to them had no doubt that punishment, as distinct from re-education and reconstruction, was a primary objective.

For large numbers of people the early post-war phase was marked by the replacement of relative prosperity with poverty, economic opportunity with central planning, and personal freedom with tight political control. In addition, repression and discrimination on the basis of class affiliation was widespread. Given these developments, many Vietnamese concluded that the situation would only deteriorate and decided to leave the country by whatever means were open to them. The outflow of refugees grew to 21,000 a year in 1977, a number that increased fivefold—to more than 100,000—by the end of 1978.[7] The trickle of refugees that had begun with the fall of Saigon had become a torrent. Nor was the situation going to improve; political developments were about to unleash a "perfect storm" on the region.

In late December 1978, Vietnamese forces invaded Cambodia (then Kampuchea) and overthrew Pol Pot and his Khmer Rouge regime. The defeat of Pol Pot brought an end to the massacres of the "Killing Fields" and provided an opportunity for tens of thousands of

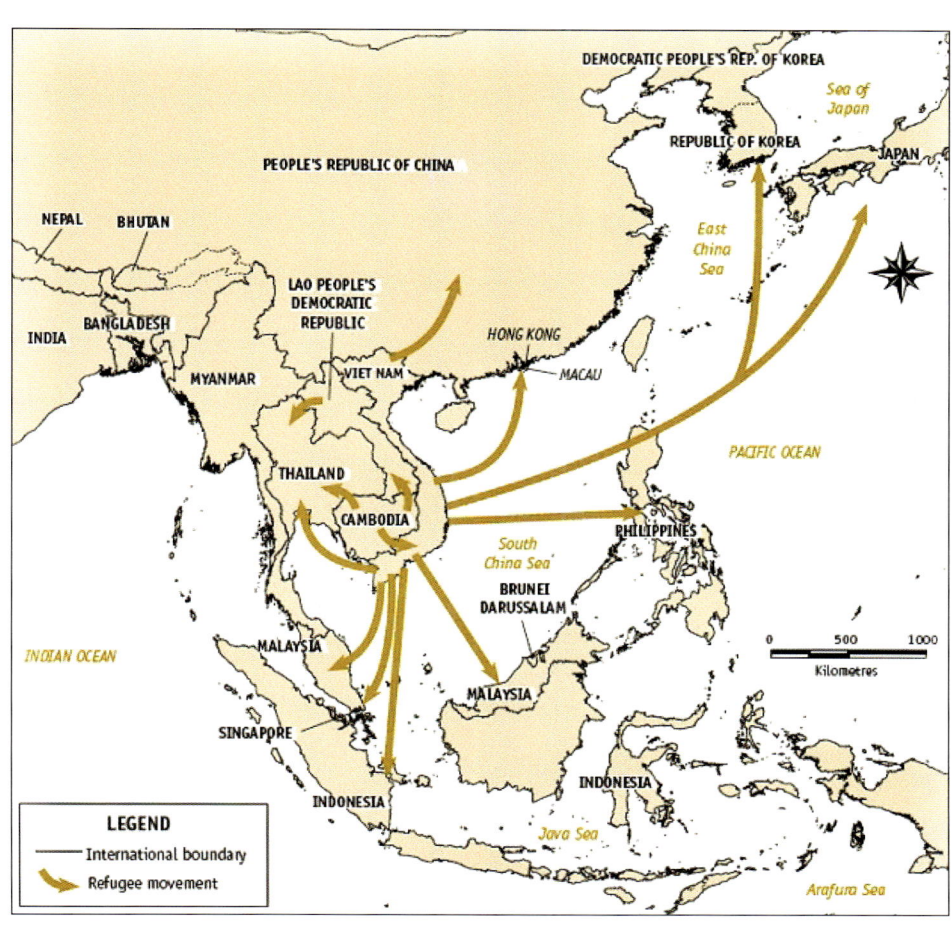

Refugee Flows, 1975-95.
Source: UNHCR: The State of the World's Refugees-2000. Map 4-1

Cambodians to flee, almost all of them overland to Thailand. The Vietnamese invasion also severely strained Hanoi's relations with China, Pol Pot's chief foreign sponsor. In response, China launched a major military incursion into Vietnam in February 1979 and a brief but intense border war took place.

Laos, as well, underwent considerable turmoil. The victory of the communist Pathet Lao, backed by North Vietnam, over the Laotian royalists in 1975 and the new regime's attempts to reshape the country along communist lines produced growing distress and impoverishment. Many of the Hmong people, Laotian highlanders who had fought alongside the Americans, fled shortly after the communist victory. By late 1978, an increasing number of lowland Laotians were also seeking refuge across the border in Thailand.

One major consequence of the Sino-Vietnamese hostilities was increased pressure on the large ethnic Chinese community (the Hoa) living in Vietnam. Already under suspicion because of their economic orientation as free market traders and merchants, the ethnic Chinese were soon stigmatized as a potential fifth column prepared to do the bidding of Vietnam's giant neighbour. Many of the ethnic Chinese had been hard hit by Hanoi's expropriation of private businesses early in 1978. The surge in anti-Hoa sentiment made an already bad situation substantially worse. Nor was it only the ethnic Chinese in the south who were affected. By the end of 1979, over a quarter of a million Vietnamese of Chinese extraction had fled north—to China—the great majority from the former North Vietnam.[8]

Chaos, brutality, war and dispossession—the horsemen of a modern apocalypse—combined to persuade tens of thousands of Southeast Asians that their only hope lay in flight. For its part, the Vietnamese government apparently decided to stop attempting to prevent large-scale departures and to acquiesce in, or actively profit from, the exodus. By the summer of 1979, people were fleeing the region by any and every means.

Cambodian Child Refugees.
Courtesy, UNHCR

In the eyes of the world, the humanitarian tragedy of 1978–79 would come to be symbolized by the "boat people": refugees of all ages and conditions crowded into flimsy vessels courageously — and desperately — risking everything on a perilous voyage to an uncertain destination. That enduring image is understandable, as the greatest proportion of the more than 300,000 Vietnamese who fled their country by sea between 1975 and 1979 [9] did so on small, flimsy craft. While the boat people's travails captured global attention, even larger numbers of "land people" hazarded everything on an often-dangerous, sometimes-fatal flight overland to Thailand. The entire region was aflame as people in their tens of thousands sought to escape from circumstances that had become intolerable. Cambodians fleeing the "killing fields", highland and lowland Laotians, ethnic Vietnamese from both North and South, and Vietnamese of Chinese extraction all contributed to a vast outpouring that would affect a dozen countries in Asia and the Pacific.

REGIONAL RESPONSES

The flight of some intrepid exiles took them as far afield as South Korea and Australia, covering vast distances with only the slenderest resources. Geography, however, dictated that over 95 percent would seek asylum in half a dozen jurisdictions closer to home. Thailand was particularly affected; a non-communist country bordering directly on Laos and Cambodia, it was the only feasible destination for those who fled overland. In addition, Malaysia, Indonesia and Singapore to the south, the Philippines to the west, and Hong Kong to the north all witnessed the arrival of tens of thousands of people, often in appalling circumstances.

Keo Khamphoune and her children in a Thai refugee camp.
Courtesy, Bounkeo Khamphoune

Children in a Hong Kong refugee camp.
Courtesy, UNHCR

In the immediate post-Vietnam War period, refugees were relatively few and seem to have met no insurmountable obstacles in building new lives for themselves, within or beyond the region. By 1978, however, the patience and resources of the host countries were close to exhaustion. In addition to the huge demands that the rising tide of refugees placed on scarce national resources, each government had reasons sufficient—in its own eyes—to adopt an increasingly tough stance toward those seeking asylum. The human torrent showed no signs of abating and was threatening to become a flood. Permanent resettlement beyond the region was slow and limited. International humanitarian assistance was inadequate to deal with the growing scope of the problem.

The rising power of Vietnam—with the largest and most effective military forces in the area and a demonstrated readiness to use them—made its neighbours cautious. In several countries, the influx of large numbers of foreigners threatened to swamp complex and often fragile accommodations among different ethnic and cultural communities. In addition, the absorptive capacity of several jurisdictions—notably Singapore and Hong Kong, with their extremely high population densities—was clearly limited.

Boat people off the Malaysian coast, 1978.
Courtesy, UNHCR

The mix of motives and justifications varied from one government to another. Collectively, however, the countries in which the refugees first sought asylum were becoming increasingly vocal. The problem was not of their making, they asserted; it had already outgrown their capacities, and the international community at large had to mobilize to deal with the crisis.

By the fall of 1978, regional frustration and impatience had reached the tipping point. Refugees, whether arriving by land or by sea, were being characterized primarily as actual or potential security threats. Herded into camps, often barely able to meet their most basic needs, the refugees entered a political limbo in which they could do little but wait on others to decide their fate.

A local rescue.
Courtesy, UNHCR

And, some started to suspect, they were the lucky ones. Singapore began to refuse to allow boat people to disembark unless they had guarantees of resettlement elsewhere within 90 days. Malaysia and Thailand resorted increasingly to "push-backs," shoving refugee craft out to sea to ensure that their passengers could not disembark. Governments also employed other measures. Far offshore, local patrol craft intercepted some refugee vessels and re-supplied them, on the condition that they sail on and make

Refugee camp scene.
Courtesy, UNHCR

no attempt to land their passengers. The "land people" were no more welcome. Although the Thai authorities did not deny them entry, the exiles were confined to camps along the border with only the most basic food, shelter and health care.

THE *HAI HONG* AFFAIR

The plight of the refugees was drawn dramatically to the world's attention and placed firmly on the international political agenda through the unlikely agency of a rusting old freighter that had been sold for scrap, the *Hai Hong*. On November 9, 1978, crammed with some 2,500 Vietnamese, the *Hai Hong* dropped anchor off the Malaysian city of Port Klang and sought permission to land its passengers. Fearful of attracting still more refugees, the Malaysians refused. The vessel, in turn, refused to leave. During the ensuing standoff, Malaysian officials denied the claims of the passengers to refugee status—on the grounds that they had bought their way out of Vietnam—and threatened to have the *Hai Hong* towed back out to sea.

The *Hai Hong*.
Courtesy, Ian Hamilton

The plight of the freighter's helpless passengers attracted worldwide media attention. Pictures of a banner hung from the ship, reading "Please Rescue Us" in English, were picked up by the international news agencies and the story was relayed around the world. With conditions aboard the overloaded freighter deteriorating, and its passengers facing probable death by drowning if the Malaysians carried out their threat, the *Hai Hong* came to represent the enormous travails of Southeast Asia. For the first time since the end of the Vietnam War, the refugees had a human face.

Global sympathy helped bring the *Hai Hong* case to an early and positive conclusion, with Canada playing a key role in the process. On November 18, Ottawa offered to take 600 of the *Hai Hong's* passengers for permanent resettlement. Ian Hamilton, whose tour as Canada's senior immigration officer in Southeast Asia spanned the 1978–79 crisis, recalls the scene vividly.

As the Malaysians would allow no one to board the *Hai Hong*, Ian and his small staff set up operations aboard a Malaysian navy vessel, to

Aboard the *Hai Hong*.
Courtesy, Ian Hamilton

which small groups of refugees were ferried for processing. The Canadians soon learned first hand of the travails of the *Hai Hong's* passengers. Yet even amid widespread suffering and deprivation, small signs of hope insinuated themselves.

Recognizing early on that he would need someone competent in several languages to assist him, Ian interviewed one of the first people to come over from the *Hai Hong*. The man was alone, he was desperate to learn the whereabouts of his family—who had fled before him—and his family name was Luu. Ian recalled that a few weeks earlier, aboard another freighter that had been grounded in Indonesia, he had selected for admission to Canada another family named Luu, comprising a woman and several young children. Pulling from his briefcase the identity photos he had taken, he showed them to the desperate man. Amazed to discover that his family had survived and had been granted admission to Canada, and that he would shortly be able to join them, the overwhelmed Mr. Luu was temporarily unable to express himself in any of the four languages that he spoke.[10]

Ian Hamilton with a refugee child.
Courtesy, Ian Hamilton

To make good on its commitment and to see to the refugees' immediate needs, the Canadian government dispatched military medical teams and aircraft to bring the refugees to their new land. Dr. Stephen Blizzard, then chief medical officer at the Canadian Forces base in North Bay, recalls that he happened to be reading about the boat people when his superior called. Was he willing to participate in "Operation Magnet," the military's designation for the exercise? Sixteen days later, after an odyssey of over 30,000 kilometres, Dr. Blizzard returned to Canada knowing that he had contributed directly to the safe arrival in Canada of 604 refugees. He also knew that had the standoff lasted much longer, the consequences for the refugees would have been dire; hunger, thirst and exhaustion had already depleted their reserves. The refugees' resolve and determination deeply impressed him. Despite their ordeal, they expressed neither recrimination nor regret; rather, self-discipline and gratitude prevailed during the long, two-day flight to Canada.[11]

Other immigrant-receiving nations soon followed Canada's lead. In short order, the refugees aboard the *Hai Hong* were able to make their way to new lives beyond the region and the immediate crisis was over. The episode marked an important milestone in the broader Southeast Asian refugee crisis. It provided a highly visible example in which countries of temporary asylum, the United Nations High Commissioner for Refugees (UNHCR) and other international assistance organizations, and countries of permanent resettlement worked together successfully to ease the plight of the boat people. An implicit bargain had been struck—"an open door for an open shore"[12]—between the countries of temporary asylum and those of permanent resettlement.

Dr. Stephen Blizzard, November 1978.
Courtesy, Dr. Stephen Blizzard

The success was both modest and partial. In the early months of 1979, the exodus of Vietnamese, Laotians and Cambodians once again began to build. By the summer, 50,000 to 60,000 people a month were fleeing their homelands. Malaysian hostility to the refugees was such that, in June, a senior government minister publicly threatened to expel all boat people in his country and to shoot any new arrivals on sight. One contemporary account put the number whom the Malaysians towed back out to sea during the first half of 1979 at 58,000.[13]

Malaysia's treatment of the boat people was probably the most widely criticized in the international media. Several other reluctant hosts behaved in much the same fashion, however, with refusals of permission to land, push-backs and similar measures becoming increasingly common. The "land people" met with similar hostility. That same month, in what UNHCR sources described as the largest forced return ever encountered by their organization, Thai military elements forced more than 42,000 Cambodian refugees out of border camps and "down the steep mountainside at Preah Vihear into Cambodia. At least several hundred people, and possibly several thousand, were killed in the minefields below."[14] In the tide of suffering about to overwhelm the region, however, the prompt resolution of the *Hai Hong* case represented one small life raft of hope.

THE REFUGEES AND THE WORLD

The *Hai Hong* affair also brought to light the unsavoury reality of human trafficking amid the humanitarian tragedy. The rusty, dilapidated freighter that had anchored in Malaysian waters was not the first—nor would it be the last—of the "profit ships" on which some of the boat people fled. In brief, unscrupulous entrepreneurs—based chiefly in Singapore and Hong Kong—would acquire some barely seaworthy hulk for scrap, buy the active or passive support of key Vietnamese officials, load it to the gunwales with refugees able to pay their extortionate rates of passage, and sail off to dump their human cargo elsewhere in the region. It was this reality that the Malaysians used to buttress their claim that the passengers aboard the *Hai Hong* were not "real refugees." As the argument would be heard again as the crisis unfolded—and would be used elsewhere by those opposed to the large-scale resettlement of the Southeast Asian refugees—it warrants treatment in a little more depth.

Some refugees, predominantly Vietnamese of Chinese extraction, were able to flee by purchasing passage on these floating coffins. Their willingness to do so simply underlines the desperation of their plight and their readiness to make whatever sacrifice was required to escape from it. As a legal observer noted at the time, "The fact that an asylum-seeker has paid for his passage out does not prejudice his status as a refugee; people have been paying to escape oppression for centuries and others have profited thereby for as long."15

Equally clear is that the number of those who fled aboard "profit ships" was modest. Vietnam, Cambodia and Laos were war-ravaged, desperately poor countries in which very few could have paid the extortionate rates charged even if they had had access to such vessels. Between the fall of Saigon and the summer of 1979, over 1 million people fled the three countries. Even the most generous estimate of the total number of refugees carried on all known "profit ships" can account for only a small fraction of those who left.

Most refugees made every effort to escape with whatever valuables they had. In a very few cases, some were able to smuggle significant wealth out with them. In the overwhelming majority of instances, however, such resources were pitiably few, quickly expended during the flight and all too often stripped from the refugees by force. While the *Hai Hong* was instrumental in gaining world attention for the plight of the refugees, it was in many respects atypical. Far

Refugees and their craft.
Courtesy, UNHCR

more representative of the maritime exodus was a small, flimsy coastal craft, inadequate for ocean travel, filled to overflowing with those prepared to entrust their fate to the capricious waters of the South China Sea.

The observation applies with particular force to the refugees who resettled in Canada. Of the 60,000 refugees who arrived in 1979–80, almost 75 percent were classified as "small boat escapees." Of the remainder, 24 percent had fled overland to Thailand. Similarly, the overwhelming majority were from modest backgrounds: over 90 percent reported having secondary education or less, while those with managerial or professional qualifications—in areas such as science and engineering, teaching, medicine and health—accounted for under 5 percent of the total.[16] Characterization of the refugees as economic migrants who left their country to pursue richer opportunities elsewhere—a line repeatedly taken by Vietnamese government officials and their allies elsewhere—was a cruel caricature of reality.

Flight overland was a difficult and often dangerous enterprise. Across wide swaths of Cambodia, and to some extent of Laos, social

Adrift, at night, on the South China Sea.
Courtesy, UNHCR

order had virtually disappeared. Refugees were at the mercy of anyone with a gun and for some that "mercy" proved lethal. For many, the flight to Thailand would be less harrowing than the experiences that awaited them. The Thai authorities were at best ambivalent toward the exiles and often openly hostile. New arrivals were interned in detention camps, operated initially by the interior ministry and later by the armed forces. Unhappily, some camps provided no haven at all. "Once in Thai camps," ran one contemporary account, "refugees were often robbed and raped by guards or other refugees."[17]

While the sufferings of the land people were widespread, the travails of the boat people were immense. Crowded aboard their frail craft, refugees often set out with only the barest of supplies of food, water and fuel, few navigational aids, and only a general idea of the route they should take. Some were picked up by passing ocean going vessels; many more were not.

Those who ran into trouble could expect little assistance from any quarter. Many fell victim to the storms for which the South China Sea is notorious. Even more lethal were the pirates who infested the southern escape routes. Operating with virtual impunity—and, some thought, with the acquiescence of local regimes who saw in them a means of frightening off further

Bleak conditions in the refugee camps.
Courtesy, Ian Hamilton

Rescue at sea.
Courtesy, UNHCR

refugees—pirate vessels attacked routinely and repeatedly. The refugees were stripped of their possessions and, sometimes, their lives. Many women and girls were raped, and some were abducted. Some refugee craft suffered multiple attacks and were so thoroughly picked over that even their engines were stolen, leaving them to float helplessly on the high seas. American navy vessels in the area encountered the aftermath of such attacks so frequently that they developed their own grim acronym for the fate of such craft: RPM, for rape, pillage and murder. It became the epitaph for many vessels that set out from Vietnam.

Between hope and despair.
Courtesy, UNHCR

Nor was all of the violence perpetrated by unknown "pirates." In the summer of 1979, reports emerged of an ill-fated boatload of refugees making for the Philippines whose craft was driven aground by bad weather in the Vietnamese-controlled Spratly Islands. Philippine marines reported hearing artillery, mortar and machine-gun fire from Vietnamese forces on shore. Of the 93 refugees aboard the craft, eight survived. Among the 85 who fell to the guns or drowned, over half were said to have been children.[18]

No one knows how many boat people lost their lives in the exodus. Some place the toll between one third and one half of those who fled Vietnam. Based on conversations with survivors and international officials, along with his own observations, Ian Hamilton believes that one third of those who set out were lost at sea.[19] Australia's minister of immigration at the time repeatedly estimated that about half the boat people died in transit. "We are looking," he said in the summer of 1979, "at a death rate of between 100,000 and 200,000 in the last four years."[20] Others have suggested a sharply lower figure, largely on the grounds that refugee vessels making for Hong Kong—who accounted for perhaps a quarter of all departures—had a generally easier time of it than those who fled by other routes. What is beyond dispute is that many thousands of those who set out were never seen again, victims of misadventure, inadequate supplies, the violence of the elements and human predators.

Whether they had fled by land or by sea, by the summer of 1979 the refugees faced a common fate. Oppressed in their countries of origin, violated and slaughtered in their flight, greeted with hostility and imprisonment when they were able to obtain tenuous asylum, the refugees were truly "the wretched of the earth."

The international news media were instrumental in first placing, and then keeping, the plight of the refugees before the conscience of the world. Vivid, harrowing tales of individual suffering, of perils met and overcome with great courage and endurance, and of the growing dimensions of the tragedy appeared with increasing frequency on the television screens and in the newspapers of the western world. Governments had begun to address the issue, but

Escape by any and every means.
Courtesy, UNHCR

the dramatic news stories that appeared throughout the industrialized democracies certainly accelerated their efforts.

The political context was hardly propitious. Memories of the Vietnam War were fresh. Vietnam was accused of exploiting the refugees for political purposes; of turning its unwanted citizens into its most profitable export; and of attempting to destabilize its non-communist neighbours, subvert their governments and hamper their development. Vietnam rejected all such accusations and charged it was being vilified no matter what it did—when it prevented people from leaving and when it later decided to allow those who wanted to depart to do so.

While the political debate ground on, the backdrop of refugee suffering continued to darken. A growing chorus of influential voices in the West called on their governments to deal directly with the increasingly urgent humanitarian crisis. As the French philosopher Jean-Paul Sartre—no friend of American policy in Southeast Asia—put it in an appeal for the French government to aid the refugees: "Some of them have not always been on our side, but for the moment we are not interested in their politics, but in saving their lives. It is a moral issue, a question of morality between human beings."[21]

The immediate trigger for international action was the adoption of a common policy approach by five of the six major countries of first refuge. In late June 1979, Indonesia, Malaysia, the Philippines, Singapore and Thailand issued a joint communiqué warning that they "had reached the limit of their endurance and [had] decided that they would not accept any new arrivals."[22] In response, the UNHCR convened a meeting the following month to head off the further deterioration of an already grim situation. Representatives of 65 countries attended and, for the first time, a coordinated international response began to emerge.

Two days before the event, as Flora MacDonald has already noted, Canada announced a dramatic increase in the number of refugees it was prepared to resettle, and other countries of permanent resettlement soon followed suit. The number of worldwide resettlement pledges more than doubled. Vietnam undertook to try to prevent illegal departures and to establish orderly departure programs. Countries of first asylum abandoned their anti-refugee rhetoric, and several pledged to streamline their own refugee processing procedures. The resources of the UNHCR, which provided for the immediate needs of many of the refugees once they had reached safety, were increased.

While the Geneva Conference of July 20–21, 1979, by no means solved the problem of Southeast Asian refugee flows, it did establish the bases for resolving the 1978–79 phase of the crisis.

The issue would remain on the international agenda for many years and would evolve in new and unexpected directions. A sudden surge of departures in the late 1980s led to a second Geneva conference in 1989. The Comprehensive Plan of Action adopted at that meeting, as well as political and economic developments within the region itself, gradually brought the crisis "to a relatively humane end," in the words of the UNHCR.[23] Such was the magnitude of the refugee movement that its consequences would continue to reverberate across the globe. Between 1975 and 1997, almost 2 million Vietnamese, Laotians and Cambodians were permanently resettled beyond the region, predominantly in North America, Western Europe and Australia. How one Canadian community responded to the moral, political and practical challenges posed by the 1978–79 phase of the crisis is the central theme of the pages that follow.

CHAPTER 3

PROJECT 4000: ORIGINS

...there can never really be peace and joy for me until there is peace and joy finally for you too.

—Frederick Buechner

THE CANADIAN CONTEXT

Of the 2 million Vietnamese, Cambodians and Laotians resettled beyond the region between 1975 and 1997, Canada took in slightly over 10 percent. Between 1975 and 1980, with 24 million nationals, Canada resettled 74,000 refugees, achieving the highest refugee-to-population ratio of any of the Western countries of permanent resettlement.[1] Such was our performance that, as earlier noted, in 1986 the UNHCR awarded its Nansen Medal to the people of Canada, the only time an entire country has been so recognized.

The Nansen Medal, currently known as the Nansen Refugee Award.
Courtesy, UNHCR.

Shared values, rather than national interests, drove Canada's response to the refugee crisis. We had not fought in the Vietnam War (a stance popular among most Canadians); trade, investment and cultural links with the region were modest to non-existent; and Canadian citizens of Southeast Asian extraction were few. Moreover, popular attitudes toward the crisis were, at best, mixed.[2] The anti-immigrant sentiment that rises and falls with the weakness and strength of Canada's economic performance remained potent.

Despite the paucity of our tangible interests, our shared national values urged the case for action. Giving asylum to those at risk and integrating new arrivals into Canadian society were established public policies that enjoyed substantial—though not universal—public support. In the post-World War II era, though not previously, the country had accepted substantial numbers of refugees along with traditional immigrants. Hungarians, Ugandan Asians, Chileans and Lebanese, among others, had entered the country seeking refuge from persecution or civil strife. The sufferings of those caught up in the humanitarian crisis unfolding half a world away resonated strongly with ordinary Canadians.

Further, little-noticed but important changes had been introduced in Canada's immigration legislation shortly before the Southeast Asian crisis hit. Prior to the introduction of the *Immigration Act* of 1978 refugee flows were treated as exceptional events – despite the large numbers sometimes involved – and dealt with through a combination of *ad hoc* political and administrative measures. The new *Act* provided, for the first time, that refugees who met internationally accepted criteria could be treated as a separate class of immigrants and their processing streamlined. Certain vulnerable groups—as distinct from individuals—could be "designated" by the government, facilitating admission on humanitarian grounds. The *Act* also greatly expanded the grounds for the sponsorship of refugees by private groups and organizations. As the country geared up to convert good intentions into practical assistance, the legal and administrative foundations for doing so were already in place.

The news media exercised a positive and powerful influence on developments. While the plight of the refugees had long been on the international agenda, intense media coverage raised its profile among governments and electorates alike and stressed the need for immediate action. The media were the sources on which individuals and organizations alike relied for information and interpretation. They were also the key instruments for mobilizing and amplifying opinion. Their efforts would have been fruitless, however, had the suffering of the refugees not touched a chord with Canadian opinion leaders across the country.

Official Canadian policy evolved as the crisis unfolded. In December 1978—immediately after the *Hai Hong* incident—Canada announced that it would accept up to 5,000 Southeast Asian claimants as part of its global refugee intake in 1979. The election of a new federal government led by Joe Clark and a rapidly worsening regional situation prompted a re-evaluation. Within days of the new government's assumption of power in June 1979, the target was raised to 7,000 and then 8,000.[3] Following the Group of Seven Tokyo Summit, as Flora MacDonald has described, the new goal was re-examined. On July 18, the Clark government announced that Canada was prepared to take up to 50,000 refugees for permanent resettlement by the end of 1980, a six-fold increase. In April 1980, the goal was again raised, to 60,000.

The political courage of the Clark government deserves comment. The radically increased target of 50,000 was well beyond the expectations of even the most vocal activists. Had the new administration wanted to keep Canada on the sidelines, it could have easily appealed to the 50 percent of Canadians who, in a February 1979 poll, had opposed raising the goal to 5,000. Instead, federal resources were deployed quickly to give effect to Canada's sharply higher target; a wide range of agreements and arrangements were put into place with provincial governments and organizations; and individual officials often took the lead in specific refugee assistance initiatives. The policy, however, was grounded on the vigorously expressed desires of ordinary Canadians. In Flora MacDonald's assessment, Project 4000—taking place in the very city in which policy was debated—and parallel initiatives elsewhere were extremely useful in persuading skeptical or reluctant federal elements to act.[4]

Beyond the many public calls for action was an impressive readiness on the part of tens of thousands of Canadians to step up to the plate. By the end of 1980, more than 7,600 private sponsorship groups had emerged across the country. Through their actions, 34,000 people—over half of the refugee intake—were resettled in every province and territory.

While the backgrounds and motivations of the activists varied widely, some generalizations are possible. Faith-based communities were front and centre. Some 65 percent of all private sponsorships were organized through religious organizations. Four Christian denominations (Catholic, Mennonite, Christian Reformed and United Church) collectively accounted for almost half of the total number of privately sponsored refugees resettled in Canada.[5] Jewish Canadians acted in exemplary fashion, as individuals and as a group. Jewish communities were active in pro-refugee organizations across the country and sponsored significant numbers of new arrivals. Canada's ethnic Chinese and Vietnamese organizations mobilized quickly and effectively, as did several other communities. Spiritual and religious traditions, humanitarian values, historic memories of persecution and ethnic identification all played their part in moving ordinary Canadians, most with no direct links to the refugees, to act.[6]

While Canadians' outpouring of compassion and support was broad and deep, generous impulses often dissipate in the absence of some means to direct and encourage them. Across the country, individuals stepped forward to provide such leadership. In Ottawa, one person stood out among the many, giving voice to the desire to help, building and sustaining the impulse, and creating a vehicle for its expression. That person was the city's 52nd mayor, Marion Dewar.

MAYOR MARION DEWAR

A long-delayed getaway, a rainy Laurentian weekend and a television set flickering in the background all had a role to play in the genesis of Project 4000.

In June 1979, Marion and her husband Ken left Ottawa for a weekend break at a Laurentian hotel a few hours from the city. They had planned their getaway for months, only to put it on hold each time they were about to leave as one or the other attended to some unavoidable duty in the capital.

Ottawa's Marion Dewar.
Courtesy, Lynn Ball/Ottawa Citizen. Reprinted by permission.

Even when the opportunity finally materialized, the gods frowned; the rain started early and continued without letup all weekend.[7]

To pass the time, the Dewars began playing bridge with another couple staying at the hotel. A television set in the background provided a minor diversion between rounds. As the weekend progressed, all four players found themselves increasingly drawn to the graphic coverage the television provided of the humanitarian tragedy unfolding half a world away. On the long drive back to Ottawa, Marion and Ken could talk of little else. The magnitude of the problem was immense and the suffering of individual refugees appalling. That the boat people were being pushed back out to sea even as they were in sight of land seemed to take cruelty to new depths. Both felt the crisis as an affront to their personal values. The question was, "What can we do?"

Over the next several days, the Dewars discussed the refugee crisis with a few close friends who, like them, were practising Christians. While all were distressed by the plight of the refugees, most saw no immediate way to provide tangible assistance. Unable to rid her mind of the horrific images, the mayor invited a number of local religious and community leaders, and the federal immigration minister, to a private meeting at City Hall. While unable to attend in person, the immigration minister agreed to send a senior official to represent him.

The meeting took place on June 27. Can Le attended the session in his capacity of president of the Vietnamese Community Association. Can had come to Canada on a scholarship in 1963 and had gone on to earn two master's degrees and a doctorate before joining the federal public service as an economist. As the Southeast Asian crisis deepened, he became more directly involved in the life of the tiny Vietnamese community then living in Ottawa. He recalls being deeply impressed by the range of groups represented at the June 27 meeting, and by their enthusiasm for practical action. Equally impressive was the mayor. In his assessment, Marion Dewar's political leadership was the key element that moved the initiative forward.[8]

As the meeting progressed, it quickly became evident that few of those present—other than the minister's representative—thought that the federal government was doing enough. In response to the criticism, the federal official argued that Canada had already accomplished a good deal. The intake target had just been raised to 8,000 refugees for the 1979 calendar year and, six months into the year, 4,000 had already been selected. Struck by the gap between the magnitude of the crisis as portrayed by the media and the official's comments, Marion Dewar said, "Fine. We'll take the other 4,000." Surely, she thought, integrating a few thousand people into a city of more than 300,000 would not be terribly difficult.

The comment was offered spontaneously, less as a serious proposal than as an expression of dissatisfaction with the modest size of Canada's official target. The discussion moved on to other aspects of the crisis and the meeting ground to a close. However, the exchange had crystallized the mayor's thinking. Project 4000, a commitment to resettle large numbers of Southeast Asian refugees in Ottawa, had been born.

Reviewing events with her advisors, Marion Dewar quickly reached two conclusions. City council approval was urgent. She consulted informally with a number of council members and arranged for the matter to be submitted to council at its next scheduled meeting, on July 4. Equally clear was the need to consult the public at large. Project 4000 as an initiative would stand or fall on the strength of the broad public support it attracted. A process was needed—and quickly—to gauge the willingness of Ottawans to get involved, and to ensure that the City could deliver on any commitments made. A planning group of two dozen persons of widely differing backgrounds was formed to examine the various issues involved in a large-scale resettlement project and, more immediately, to organize a public rally on the initiative.

The press soon got wind of these events. Later the same day, reporters asked the mayor about her meeting. The plight of the refugees had been the main subject of discussion, she responded, then added, "We are thinking of taking 4,000." On June 28, the *Ottawa Citizen* ran a brief account under the heading "Ottawa readies haven plan for 4,000 refugees," while the now-defunct *Ottawa Journal* carried a one-paragraph story entitled, "Dewar wants city to take more refugees." Not only had Project 4000 seen the light of day, it was showing every sign of toddling right out of the nursery.

The initiative quickly developed momentum. The same day that the papers broke the story, the planning group met at a local church to begin work. The following day, June 29, Mayor Dewar held a press conference. Describing Project 4000 as a response to "a groundswell of enthusiasm and support from city residents," she announced that a public meeting would take place at Lansdowne Park on July 12. Her office had been inundated, she told reporters, with calls from Ottawans offering food, clothing and shelter. People wanted to give practical assistance to the refugees but had no means to do so. The meeting on July 12 was being organized to gauge the depth of public concern and to give potential volunteers and donors a chance to come forward.

She stressed the urgency of the need for action. Responding to a comment that perhaps more planning and assessment should have been done before a target was set, she said, "Yes. We could have had more information if we waited. We would have had a better indication if we'd studied the situation for two and a half years, but in the meantime, a lot of people would be at the bottom of the ocean." [9] Whatever the political risks she ran in advancing the initiative, she was prepared to assume them.

The mayor also used the press conference to urge a stronger national response. She challenged the mayors of other Canadian cities to launch similar consultations with their citizens, arguing that municipal leaders could serve as catalysts for effective action by their communities. Because of Marion Dewar's political profile, she was able to attract national attention to a quintessentially local initiative, and thereby make Project 4000 an important and influential stimulus in the broader Canadian grassroots response.

Immediate response to the launch of Project 4000 was strongly, though not universally, positive. Public and media commentary was broadly supportive, though the planned public meeting loomed as the real test for the project. The optimists thought that the event could easily attract several hundred people, all of them presumably wanting detailed information on what they were being asked to take on.

Despite the generally positive public reaction, some doubted the city's ability to provide jobs and accommodation for large numbers of newcomers. One of the papers editorialized that Canada would be more effective by increasing its assistance to the region and promoting a political settlement than by encouraging large-scale resettlement schemes. Some criticisms shaded into overt racism, with concerns raised at the prospect of fundamental changes being made to the composition of the Canadian population. Some would have been genuinely amusing had they not been so ill intentioned. Marion Dewar recalls taking one phone call in which the caller threatened to kidnap her, tie her up, take her up to Parliament Hill and feed her Chinese food "until she exploded."

In advancing the proposal to bring in up to 4000 refugees, Mayor Dewar clearly acted from the depths of her own convictions. As Russ Mills, then editor of the *Ottawa Citizen*, puts it, "Marion acted because she thought it was the right thing to do. She did not do it for political gain."[10] In fact, the risk lay in taking action. The politically "safe" course for her would have been—as some civic leaders did elsewhere—to step back and say that the problem, while deeply regrettable, lay beyond her jurisdiction.

Other observers have offered similar assessments. "With Marion," recalls Richard Hardy, a professor at Saint Paul University, "there was never any question of self-aggrandizement or personal or political gain. She set a wonderful personal example and people responded accordingly."[11] Nailed firmly to the mast of the mayor's high-profile plan to help strangers half a world away was her political reputation. Success or failure depended heavily on the initiative finding some resonance among the citizens of Ottawa. The early signs were largely positive. Still, until the Lansdowne Park rally allowed ordinary people to voice their opinions, it was an open question whether Project 4000 would prove an effective grassroots social movement or a major political embarrassment.

First Steps

The two weeks between the mayor's press conference and the planned public consultation on July 12 passed in a blur. Michael Lubbock, a retired banker who had participated in refugee relief operations in Europe immediately after World War II, came forward to serve as interim coordinator. (Although he would later step aside when the position became permanent, Michael remained an active and constructive influence within the organization.) The mayor found him temporary office accommodation in City Hall, provided him with the essentials needed to begin operations and devoted her political skills to winning the support of her city council colleagues for Project 4000.

On July 4, city council unanimously endorsed the initiative and allocated $25,000 to help meet start-up costs. Five council members, including the mayor, also agreed collectively to sponsor a refugee family. The City's employees were no less positive, responding "magnificently"—to use the mayor's term—to the growing number of unusual tasks, from processing unsolicited financial donations to dealing with requests for information on a wide variety of matters.

The citizens' planning group, expanded in size and function, swung into high gear. Alan Breakspear—a federal public servant with a longstanding interest in immigration and refugee policy, who would succeed Michael Lubbock as Project 4000's coordinator—led the group. Early on, he put forward a "needs assessment" as a means of focusing attention on the issues that were bound to arise. The assessment led to the creation of nine separate sub-groups that, in turn, would become the eventual organizational units of Project 4000.

Simply listing the titles of the sub-groups demonstrates the scope of the challenges expected to occur: Education and Training, Health Services, Employment, Accommodation, Government Relations, Private Sponsorship, Settlement and Adaptation, Funding, and Media Relations. Volunteers came forward to staff each one.

Alan and his colleagues recognized that they could not possibly master the intricacies of all of these areas prior to July 12; their immediate aim was to develop preliminary answers to the dozens of probable questions. In addition, the organization of the rally itself required a good deal of time and energy. The logistics of a session expected to attract several hundred had to be arranged, the program of events organized, and 100 volunteers trained to staff the information booths that would be used to deal with specific expressions of interest.[12]

One other early step deserves mention. As a municipal politician who had taken her share of media criticism over the years, Marion Dewar was acutely aware of the power of the press in shaping the public agenda and moulding public opinion. On July 5, she met privately with representatives of the local media to present her case for urgent action and, if possible, to enlist their support. She clearly had some success, for in the following weeks and months press coverage of Project 4000, while not uncritical, was generally sympathetic.

Russ Mills, the *Citizen's* editor, was particularly touched by her words. After the meeting, it occurred to him that there were probably a good number of Ottawans who would like to help but lacked the contacts and mechanisms to do so. Perhaps his newspaper could help to match potential sponsors with sponsorship groups needing additional members. When he returned to his office, he raised the idea with his colleagues, who quickly agreed. "It was an unusual step for a newspaper to take," he recalls. "As journalists, we try to maintain a certain distance from political initiatives, to preserve our capacity to provide the public with independent commentary. In this case, however, we thought that the circumstances were such as to warrant an extraordinary response."[13]

On July 7, Russ wrote in the paper that although the *Citizen* could not play an official role in Project 4000, it planned to make two specific contributions. "First, we will sponsor a refugee family ourselves and we invite other local businesses to follow our example. Names of all businesses that agree to sponsor

THE REFUGEES

Citizen readers have a chance to help the boat people. If you would like to help sponsor a refugee family, fill out the form below and mail to **The Citizen**. *We'll divide sponsors into groups of about 30 households and publish the names of all members of each group so you'll know the other members of your sponsoring group. Sponsorship is a moral and financial commitment not to be taken lightly. Please do not send the form unless you are seriously interested.*

I want to help sponsor a refugee family

Name...
Address..
Phone..

Mail to: Refugees, The Citizen, 1101 Baxter Rd., Ottawa, K2C 3M4
(or deliver to The Citizen front desk)

The *Ottawa Citizen's* sponsorship form.
Courtesy, The Ottawa Citizen. Reprinted by permission.

a refugee family will be published….in what we hope will be a growing list."[14]

Of equal significance, the paper offered to serve as a communications link through which would-be sponsors could form their own groups. The form reproduced in this chapter appeared in the paper on several occasions in the following weeks.

The *Citizen's* initiative was important for several reasons. It raised the public profile of the issue sharply, endorsed the sponsorship campaign as a worthy undertaking and extended the opportunity to participate well beyond Ottawa's city limits to the paper's entire circulation area.

THE LANSDOWNE PARK RALLY

As planned, the program for the event was straightforward. Alan Breakspear would serve as master of ceremonies. Marion Dewar, and a few prominent religious and community leaders, would briefly address the crowd. Folk singer

Vietnamese singers at the Lansdowne Park rally.
Courtesy, Eleanor Ryan.

Bruce Cockburn and a choir of Vietnamese children would provide music. In addition, individuals with first-hand knowledge of the situation in Southeast Asia would speak directly about the refugee crisis. Information booths on the various facets of the program would be strategically located throughout the hall. The organizers looked to the event as a means of assessing the depth of public support for Project 4000 and, with luck, of adding to the stream of private offers of assistance that were already flowing in from across the city.

As professional event organizers and active political supporters of Marion Dewar, Barb and Dan Gamble had volunteered to look after the logistics of the rally. As Barb describes the preparations: "We put six hundred chairs out in Exhibition Hall. By the time the meeting started, hundreds more chairs were pulled out, we had extended into the next hall and the aisles were filled with people!"[15] No one knows precisely how many attended; estimates range from 2,300 to 3,000. By any standard, it was a far greater response than the organizers had expected to see. Sue and George Pike, who had also volunteered

Bruce Cockburn at the Lansdowne Park rally.
Courtesy, Eleanor Ryan.

to help, agree. "We kept opening more doors", recalls Sue " to more halls to accommodate the people who kept crowding in."

Even more striking was the sense that the crowd had already made up its mind. George remembers that "No persuasion was necessary. There were no searching questions. People just wanted to pitch right in."[16]

If the organizers were impressed by the size of the turnout, they were amazed by the collective determination to act. Marion Dewar later noted, "We went into the meeting to determine *whether* we should proceed. We came out it focused on *how* we were going to do it." For George Pike, the event was "a love-in."

Participants in the Lansdowne Park rally.
Courtesy, Eleanor Ryan.

Will you hear us?
Courtesy, Eleanor Ryan.

Something magical seems to have happened that night. The Roman Catholic Archbishop of Ottawa, Joseph Aurèle Plourde—already in the process of sponsoring a Cambodian orphan—expressed his admiration and love for the people of a city that would respond openheartedly to the suffering of strangers. Rabbi Don Gerber of Temple Israel, recalling the unwillingness of most Western countries—including Canada—to open their doors to Jewish refugees on the eve of World War II, held up Project 4000 as an historic opportunity to learn from the past and do better. Bishop William Robinson, the city's senior Anglican prelate, praised the mayor for her initiative and exhorted the crowd to show their support. They promptly did so by rising to their feet and giving her a standing ovation.

Marion Dewar addressing the rally.
Courtesy, Eleanor Ryan.

Marion Dewar certainly felt the current. "There is something genuine happening here," she told her audience. "But…it is not my project. It was your council that voted unanimously to support Project 4000 and you who came out tonight."[17] The crowd soon made it clear that they had come for more than speeches and songs. Spontaneously, people began to make their way to the information booths, not for details on the project but to see how they could help. In one night, Project 4000 saw the number of specific offers of assistance virtually double, and more would flow in during the weeks ahead. Such was the response that it took volunteers a full day to record and organize all of the pledges and donations made at the rally.

The outcome was all the more remarkable because sponsorship represented a substantial commitment. Sponsors assumed a legally binding obligation to care for the individual or family whom they took on for up to one year. The estimated cost of sustaining a single family for 12 months was between $9,000 and $12,000 (in 1979 dollars), a significant engagement on behalf of total strangers. Ottawans had made plain that they were prepared to open their pocketbooks as well as their hearts to the refugees.

A luminous memory for participants, the rally at Lansdowne Park was a defining moment in the evolution of Project 4000. Whether the evening was touched by grace, magic or simply solidarity with strangers half a world away mattered little. The mayor had given voice to the plight of the refugees, sketched a vision of how ordinary people might help and called on her city to rise to the occasion. Ottawa had responded with a depth and a passion that surprised even the most optimistic. Rabbi Gerber describes the event in the following terms. The rally "overwhelmed the organizers, the mayor's committee, the neighbourhood 'adopters,' all volunteers, the Vietnamese refugees already living in our midst…it overwhelmed us all with emotion. At the heart of that emotion was that we were about to achieve much more than we thought we could. The Lansdowne Park rally made us all believers in our best selves."[18]

STRUCTURE AND RESOURCES

In less than three weeks, Project 4000 had grown from an offhand comment at a private meeting to a full-blown social movement. It was time to put into place the structures and resources needed to ensure that the groundswell of public enthusiasm was channelled to achieve tangible results.

Documents were quickly drafted to establish Project 4000 as a non-profit charitable corporation and submitted to the provincial authorities. As set out in the application for incorporation, the key objectives were as follows.

(a) To assist and encourage the settlement of refugees in and around the City of Ottawa and the Regional Municipality of Ottawa-Carleton.

(b) To assist and encourage the alleviation of suffering and restoration of dignity amongst refugees wherever possible.

(c) To develop and/or encourage and support the development of such services, programmes and activities as may be necessary and appropriate to meet the needs of refugees…and of organizations, associations and groups which undertake to sponsor or otherwise…assist such refugees.

(d) To raise…funds for the purposes of assisting refugee sponsorship and settlement programmes; of defraying the expenses of programmes…[supporting] the aims of the Corporation; and of contributing…to international relief…and development assistance….

(e) To maintain liaison and consultative relationships with the community and with Municipal, Provincial, and Federal Governments, departments and agencies so as to support and encourage...policies and programmes consistent with the aims of the Corporation.[19]

Project 4000 was to pursue its aims under the direction of a large, representative board of directors. Among those selected to serve—without remuneration—were religious leaders, public servants, lawyers, local politicians, bankers, business people, heads of ethnic associations and labour representatives. The project coordinator—the role initially taken on by Michael Lubbock and then by Alan Breakspear—would be responsible for day-to-day operations. The coordinator was to be the nucleus of a very small paid staff around which the volunteers, on whom the organization would depend heavily, would coalesce.

The Board held its first meeting on August 2, at which it reviewed the events that had led to the establishment of Project 4000, its aims, the work of the volunteer study groups that had given life to the initiative and the Board's own internal structure. Marion Dewar, as chair of the session, stressed that the objective was clear; it was "simply to try to move people in dire need to our community and to assist them to assimilate as quickly as possible."[20] The organization chart on the next page shows the initial structure and illustrates its link to the *ad hoc* working groups created during the first frantic days following the mayor's June 29 press conference.

The urgency that marked the first weeks of Project 4000 prevailed, as the first planeload of refugees was scheduled to arrive in Ottawa within days. Fortunately, the coordinating committee that had overseen the Lansdowne Park rally, and its working groups, remained active. Preparations for the arrival of large numbers of newcomers went on, even as the transition from an informal assembly of volunteers to a legally constituted charitable organization took place.

Throughout its brief life, Project 4000 relied overwhelmingly on the freely given contributions of time, energy and materials of its many supporters. Even after allowing for the dollar's greater purchasing power in 1979, the organization began operations with financial resources best described as miniscule. Ottawa city council, as earlier noted, provided an initial grant of $25,000. The public at large provided another $19,000 in unsolicited donations.

While other grants and donations would flow in over the months ahead, the budgetary resources of the organization were never more than a tiny component of the capabilities that Project 4000 succeeded in mobilizing. A local property development corporation donated office space in one of its downtown buildings. The City of Ottawa and its personnel contributed generously across the board. Health professionals throughout the city offered medical and dental services for new arrivals at no charge. Even the small core of full-time workers—which

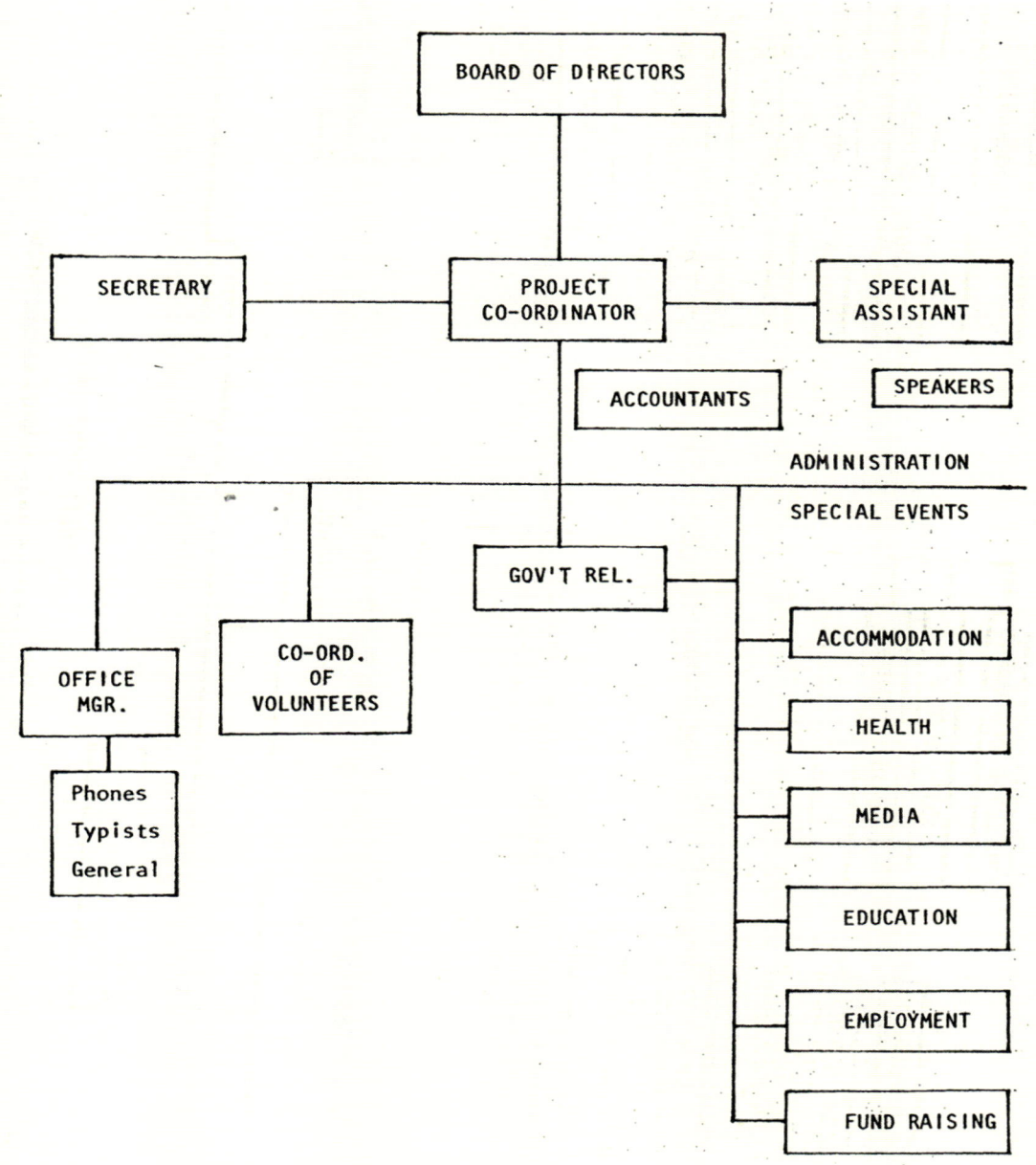

Project 4000: initial structure.
As reproduced in J. Harp's Transformation of a social movement organization

Sorting donations at the clothing depot.
Courtesy, City of Ottawa Archives, Ottawa Journal fonds

Dan Gamble recalls as never larger than four—was largely sustained by outside agencies. Alan Breakspear was seconded to Project 4000 by his home department at its expense, allowing him to devote himself entirely to the new organization. Other agencies followed suit, giving tangible support to Project 4000 by "lending" personnel for specified periods.

Beyond question, the organization's greatest resources were its volunteers. People came forward in record numbers to shoulder the dozens of tasks—from staffing furniture and clothing depots through maintaining lists of sponsorship groups to answering the phones—that needed to be performed.

The organization had to live with a number of ambiguities and uncertainties, some of which were never fully resolved. For example, was its target to resettle 4,000 refugees, or *up to* 4,000 refugees? The radically increased refugee intake target announced by the Clark government on July 18 had included a matching formula under which the federal government would support one new arrival for each one brought into Canada under private sponsorship. Should such federally supported refugees count toward Project 4000's own target? Was the Project to facilitate the work of individual sponsorship groups or to be a major actor on its own? Was its role to encourage others by example or to be a full-voiced advocate on refugee issues at large? These and related matters were debated in detail. In addition, the organization had to deal with instances — mercifully very few — in which individuals came forward to pursue their own agendas rather than the common goal, as well as its share of the personal misunderstandings and frictions inherent in organizational life.

In the end, the ambiguities and the difficulties had little impact. As Marion Dewar had noted at the first board meeting, the objective was to bring to Ottawa "people in dire need" and to help them integrate as quickly as possible. The needs of the refugees were great; the opportunity to provide tangible assistance existed; and the desire to do so — among thousands of Ottawa residents — was sharp and compelling. "Every day brought its own set of crises and issues," recalls Dan Gamble. "Problems were resolved on the fly. What we may have lacked in knowledge, we made up for in energy." Moreover, the current of public support and enthusiasm remained deep and strong. For Barb Gamble, "Project 4000 was an engine that ran on its own steam. We witnessed it. The initiative developed and sustained its own momentum."[21]

The focus of activities evolved as circumstances changed. In its initial phase, Project 4000 served chiefly to mobilize public enthusiasm for action and to provide an effective instrument for it. As hundreds of sponsorship groups came into existence, the organization concentrated on meeting their needs for information, advice, goods and services. As the groups developed their own expertise and the newcomers began to find their feet, the focus shifted again toward such questions as family reunification, secondary immigration and coordination with other agencies active in the field.

These matters, however, lay well in the future. The immediate task was clear. The first contingent of refugees was to arrive on August 6. Where were they going to live and who would look after them?

CHAPTER 4

PROJECT 4000: IMPLEMENTATION

The world is not comprehensible but it is embraceable: through the embracing of one of its beings.

—Martin Buber

WEST MEETS EAST: FIRST IMPRESSIONS

George Pike vividly recalls his first meeting with the refugee family whom he and his wife Sue had agreed to help sponsor. In September 1979, federal immigration officials informed the Pikes that "their family" had completed the long trip from the region and would arrive from Montréal the following day. Could their sponsorship group please arrange to meet them? Sue and George offered to do so and, the next morning, made their way downtown to the bus terminal.

The newcomers were not difficult to identify: a young couple, two small children and one oversize suitcase containing all of their earthly possessions. As one familiar with the pleasures of travelling with youngsters, George went over, picked up the suitcase and began to manhandle it toward the terminal exit. He had not taken more than a few steps when one of the children toddled over, firmly blocked his path and pointed downward repeatedly. George looked down. There on the bottom of the suitcase were two sturdy wheels, permitting it to be pulled rather than lifted. For a brief moment,

Arrival.
Courtesy, Drew Gragg/Ottawa Citizen. Reprinted by permission.

George thought he saw hovering over the youngster's head a cartoon balloon that read, "Nice people, these Canadians, but perhaps just a tad slow."[1]

For the newcomers, Ottawa—like Canada as a whole—was an intensely foreign environment. For most, the background cultural and even physical cues on which we all rely to navigate our daily worlds simply didn't apply. Chamroeun Lay, of Cambodian origin, came to Ottawa as a government-assisted refugee. He remembers how he and a small group of fellow Cambodians arrived in December. As the only one who spoke some English, he became the intermediary between the newcomers and their new world. He soon found there was a very large difference between knowing the words and knowing what the words really meant.

A federal immigration official met the newcomers, escorted them to a local hotel and checked them all in. Because it was late on a Friday afternoon, he told them, not much would happen until the following Monday. He gave them some food money, handed over their room keys and left.

The problem was that no one in the group had ever seen a Western-style hotel room key. Chamroeun could read the digits stamped on the tag easily enough, but they didn't correspond with any of the rooms in sight. The Cambodians were in a quandary; was this something that they were supposed to know on their own? Could they ask for help without insulting their hosts? They were extremely concerned not to give offence on their first day in their new home. Would they themselves lose face with their hosts by asking for assistance?

A hotel guest noticed their discomfort and asked if he could help. Chamroeun explained their difficulty. No problem. The first digits represented the floor on which the room was located and the second two, the room itself. And so their first obstacle was overcome through the kindness of a stranger.

After they had settled into their rooms, the Cambodians went down to the hotel dining room. Here Chamroeun received another shock. Hot dogs were one of the menu offerings. "Even though I could read the words, I had no idea what they meant. Did Canadians really eat dogs? If so, we were all going to starve!"[2] Eventually, the group made its way by public transit to Ottawa's then-tiny Chinatown, where at least the food was recognizable.

While Chamroeun now recalls these episodes with great amusement, they illustrate an important difference between the privately sponsored and government-assisted new arrivals. The government-assisted refugees were well cared for in terms of having their immediate physical needs met, and some counselling services were also provided. However, they lacked the extensive network of personal contacts and support that private sponsors could—and did—provide to "their" families.

Are we there yet?
Courtesy, M. Pinder/Ottawa Citizen. Reprinted by permission.

Few private sponsors had any particular knowledge of Southeast Asian cultures or mores, though some made efforts to learn. They had something of greater value to the newcomers: knowledge of how Canadian society and institutions operated. Privately sponsored refugees enjoyed the enormous benefit of being able to turn to a friendly and available source whenever something new and strange cropped up—as it frequently did during the early days. Whether it was grocery shopping, undergoing a medical exam, getting around an unfamiliar city or seeking out employment opportunities, privately sponsored refugees enjoyed a level of personal support well beyond that available to the government assisted. As a result, the path to self-sufficiency was certainly shorter and probably less painful for those whom a private group had taken under its wing.

Mother and child.
Courtesy, Bryce Flynn/Ottawa Citizen. Reprinted by permission.

Organizational Developments

Project 4000 had been established to mobilize support for the Southeast Asian refugees and to provide a practical means for their resettlement in Canada's capital. It succeeded massively. By December 1979, more than 300 private sponsorship groups had come into existence, sustained by between 5,000 and 6,000 area residents.[3] Several hundred volunteers also participated at the organizational level, fulfilling functions ranging from office support to the overall direction of the enterprise. A newsletter—established during the summer of 1979 and widely distributed to interested groups, media outlets and organizations— became a key means of circulating timely and relevant information to the various components of what was quickly becoming a large and complex operation.

In addition, Project 4000 generated an unprecedented flow of goods and services from the community at large. Offers of rent-free accommodation, job opportunities for newcomers, clothing and furniture, and a host of other donations came forward spontaneously from across the city and the region.

The assistance the City and its personnel extended to the new organization deserves special mention. As Ottawa's Commissioner for Community Development Robert Bailey oversaw several of the municipal units directly engaged in the challenge of resettling large numbers of newcomers. He notes that the support provided to Project 4000 included financial assistance and accounting services, legal advice, clerical support and physical services ranging from the provision of transportation to the loan of depot and storage space. Moreover the response by the municipal workforce went well beyond simple compliance with political direction. Robert and his wife Marilyn became deeply involved through their church in sponsoring and resettling a refugee family, as did many other city employees. Asked why the response was so strong he recalls "Here were these people setting out to sea in flimsy old craft in their quest for freedom. The media drew their plight forcefully to our attention and we, as ordinary citizens wanted to do something to ease their suffering." [4]

While the humanitarian crisis in Southeast Asia doubtless would have engendered some response from the people of Ottawa, Project 4000 was uniquely effective in stimulating, expanding and sustaining the local relief effort. Measured in terms of private sponsorship groups established, the response in the Ottawa area was significantly greater than the national average— clear evidence of the impact of Marion Dewar's initiative on her fellow citizens.[5]

Having surpassed its initial objective of mobilizing support for the refugees, Project 4000 needed to reassess its aims. The large number of private sponsorship groups and—more importantly—the dedication they displayed quickly persuaded the board of directors that the organization could contribute most effectively by focusing on support and coordination activities. Although Project 4000 retained most of its original structure, it morphed into a central repository—of information, goods, services and, sometimes, small-scale financial assistance—on which the hundreds of active sponsorship groups could draw to ease the resettlement of "their" refugees. The organization established and maintained a register listing offers of free or low-cost rental housing, which private sponsors could access to find suitable housing in their neighbourhoods. Similarly, central depots were established for the many spontaneous donations of furniture and clothing from the public. Sponsors and refugees were able to use the depots at no charge as the new arrivals settled into their new homes.

The organization also became an intermediary between individual sponsorship groups and the federal government regarding the administrative requirements of sponsorship. Groups had to sign their own undertakings with the immigration authorities—usually a commitment to meet all living and accommodation costs of the refugee family they had agreed to sponsor for one year—and to file reports. As a registered charity, Project 4000 was able to provide information on what was required, issue tax receipts and offer advice on general administrative questions.

Two other operational aspects deserve mention. Although Project 4000 attracted intense media attention from the beginning, it was neither the first nor the only area body actively assisting the refugees from Vietnam, Cambodia and Laos. Many faith-based communities had had programs in place well before the humanitarian crisis hit in the spring of 1979. The Ottawa Mennonite Church, for example, was particularly active on refugee issues. In addition, two well-established bodies—the Ottawa-Carleton Immigrant Services Organization (OCISO) and the Catholic Immigration Service (CIS)—operated resettlement and counselling programs for refugees as part of their wider mandates to assist immigrants; the CIS had been active in the field for decades. Project 4000 recognized the depth and range of expertise in place, and the faith-based communities actively welcomed the additional influence and resources that the Project brought to the common task.

Tony Enns, who served on the Mennonites' refugee assistance program committee, recalls that rather than a potential competitor, "We saw Project 4000 more as a kindred organization also working for the same cause."[6] Others share his view. Pat Marshall, who first became involved as a member of a local Catholic sponsorship group and subsequently joined OCISO as a full-time counsellor, remembers the working relations among the various bodies as "amazingly good." There was a singular lack of territoriality; each organization actively sought to support and strengthen the others, and the needs of the refugees remained the overriding central focus.[7]

The same concentration on the needs of the refugees permeated other Project 4000 activities as well. As noted earlier, when the Clark government announced its radically increased refugee intake target in July, it had stipulated that it would match the number of privately sponsored refugees on a one-for-one basis. As the pace of refugee selection and processing quickened, both privately sponsored and government-assisted refugees began arriving in the region in growing numbers. Should the organization limit its efforts to the privately sponsored or assist people in both categories? Project 4000 decided early on that "who was being supported by whom" was unimportant. The paramount aim was to assist the newcomers as effectively as possible to rebuild their lives in their new land.

As a result, the common services that Project 4000 provided—the furniture and clothing depots and specialized information facilities—were made freely available to anyone in need. The organization clearly had taken to heart Marion Dewar's words at the first board meeting: that Project 4000 existed simply "to move people in dire need to our community and to assist them to assimilate as quickly as possible." The lesson was well learned and never forgotten.

Within a few months, Project 4000 had settled into its role. "Project 4,000," noted a subsequent overview, " focused in early 1980 on providing support and guidance to private sponsor groups and on ensuring that refugees themselves, both privately sponsored and government sponsored, received the training, support and counselling they needed in their first few months in Canada."[8] These activities continued to evolve and expand, notably in the area of employment skills and job placement, as the resettlement and integration of the newcomers proceeded.

LOSS AND RECOVERY

Despite the deep reservoirs of goodwill and practical assistance available, many—perhaps most—refugees found the process of adapting to an entirely new society arduous and painful. The ancient Greeks thought that of all the ills to which humanity is heir, the "greatest grief" was to be deprived of one's homeland. Coming to terms with the reality and the magnitude of what had been lost required time, courage and endurance. While the refugees had escaped, they had not escaped unscathed. The wounds were deep and apt to demand recognition at any time.

Diep Trinh, his wife Tam, three children and a brother-in-law arrived in Ottawa in the summer of 1979, as Project 4000 was becoming operational. The Trinhs were unusually fortunate in that not only did Diep speak English, but a relative, Can Le, was already well established in what was to become their new home. With the assistance of Can and his wife Vuong the Trinhs found the process of resettling in Ottawa somewhat less daunting than it otherwise would have been.

A family reunion.
Courtesy, Diep Trinh.

The first winter in Canada was very hard. The cold was beyond anything the Trinhs had imagined. Moreover, the trauma of their escape was still present. Diep remembers one winter day when he and his wife had gone grocery shopping. They had stocked up on oranges, bananas and fruit of all kinds. As they had no car and had to carry their purchases some distance back to their apartment, Diep decided to try a shortcut across a snow-covered field. "A big mistake," he recalls. He had taken only a few steps when he slipped on a hidden patch of ice and sprawled headlong in the snow. As he watched the brightly coloured oranges and other memories of warmer climates disappear, he was overwhelmed by a sense of deep and irretrievable loss. It came out of nowhere and left him shaken, cold, wet and profoundly aware of how desperately far he was from everything he had once loved.

Other, happier events took place as well. Having found work as a seamstress, Tam Trinh gradually became friends with a number of her co-workers. During a casual conversation about Christmas one autumn day, a Canadian co-worker had been surprised to learn that the holiday had been widely celebrated in South Vietnam. Tam thought no more about the conversation as they all went back to work.

Some weeks later, as Christmas approached, the Trinhs heard a knock at their door. They opened

The Trinh family's first Tulip Festival.
Courtesy, Diep Trinh.

it and there was the co-worker with a large hamper of food, presents for the children and a small artificial Christmas tree. Even after the family's circumstances had improved and they had moved into their own home, Diep remembers, "we held on to that little Christmas tree for many years."[9]

Small acts of kindness sometimes had large and lasting impacts. Elizabeth Rapley had become engaged in refugee matters well in advance of Project 4000, largely because a friend had asked her to help a pregnant young Cambodian refugee find her way around Ottawa. Elizabeth and her daughter agreed and the three women became close friends. While they were visiting one day, another young Cambodian woman—also in the late stages of pregnancy—dropped in. She was obviously in some discomfort and Elizabeth, remembering what it had been like as she awaited the arrival of her own children, spontaneously reached out and massaged the young woman's lower back. The woman turned around, deeply moved. Just for a moment she had felt the presence of her own mother, swept away in the Cambodian genocide, comforting her as her time to give birth drew near. Elizabeth, who has remained close to the Cambodian community, remembers that for years afterwards, whenever they met, the woman would recall the afternoon when Elizabeth had massaged her sore back and she had been touched by a mother's hand.[10]

Liem Duong also remembers what it was like to experience the compassion of a stranger. Liem arrived in Ottawa in July 1983, part of the inflow of refugees from Vietnam, Cambodia and Laos that continued well after the formal termination of Project 4000. Although he held a degree in agricultural engineering from a Vietnamese university, he soon concluded that he was unlikely to find satisfying work without more education. Even though, as a government-assisted refugee, he qualified for an extended period of benefits, he was determined to become self-supporting as quickly as possible. Within two months of arrival, he had enrolled at Carleton University and found a job washing dishes in a restaurant. His life consisted of studying from 8 a.m. until 4:30 p.m., and then washing dishes between 5 p.m. and 1 a.m. He recalls with a smile that he "didn't have a great deal of free time."

Liem went on in due course to a highly successful career with the federal government and now holds the position of Engineering Manager with the Department of National Defence. During his early years in Ottawa, while he was still working at the restaurant, he began to suffer from serious stomach pains. Eventually, he went to a downtown clinic where the doctor on duty told

A Thanksgiving meal.
Courtesy, Ian Hamilton.

him that he had a bleeding ulcer and needed to get to a hospital right away. When she found that he planned to go by bus, she passed the hat among the clinic's staff, raised enough to cover cab fare, and insisted that he go—immediately—by taxi. He did so and later, after he had recovered, returned to say thanks. The doctor had moved on, leaving no forwarding address, and he had to content himself with making a financial contribution to the clinic's operations.[11]

Inevitably, there were missteps and false starts. Scottish-born Phyllis Hardie belonged to a church group in the Aylmer area that had undertaken to sponsor a Vietnamese family comprising two adults and three children. She remembers being very impressed by the work ethic of the parents and the demeanour of the children, one of whom remained close friends with her own son through elementary and secondary school.

Learning that the mother of the family spoke no English, Phyllis volunteered to teach her. A few sessions into the training, she realized that her student was picking up her own accent along with the language. "After hearing her pronounce the word 'currrtain' a few times, I realized I was doing her no favours," she recalls. Adapting to life in Canada as a member of an Asian community was one thing; going through life as a member of an Asian community who spoke English with a distinct Scottish burr was something else again. Phyllis decided she could be more effective in other ways and another language teacher was found.[12]

Gradually the refugees began to put down roots in their new land. Winter was always memorable, particularly during the early years. Nancy and Doug Umbach had been engaged for years in refugee relief and international adoption issues through their local Baptist congregation in Hanover, Ontario. When they moved to Ottawa in 1980, Nancy quickly became active with Project 4000. She remembers that newcomers would often ask, "You don't go outside in winter, do you?"

"Yes, we do, but we dress properly for the cold," she would reply.

"But you don't really go outside, do you?"

The first skate on the Rideau Canal was "always an adventure."[13] Still, with persistence, determination and some encouragement from their Canadian friends, the newcomers adapted to winter. Some even learned to enjoy—or least tolerate—it.

A pick-up volleyball game.
Courtesy, Larry MacDougal/Ottawa Citizen. Reprinted by permission.

Winter 101.
Courtesy, Bounkeo Khamphoune.

Evolution of a Mandate

Despite the impact Project 4000 had—and continues to have—on the capital region, the operational phase of its existence lasted little more than 18 months. In the spring of 1980, Project 4000 was reorganized and an executive committee of the board of directors was created to deal with changing circumstances. By the summer of 1980, it was clear that the initial needs for which Project 4000 had been established had largely been met. The refugees were getting on with the task of rebuilding their lives. Although full integration into mainsteam Canadian life would require years rather than months, the challenges the Vietnamese, Cambodians and Laotians faced were increasingly similar to those all newcomers encountered. Similarly, the private sponsorship groups were either approaching the term of their engagement or had developed sufficient expertise that they were able to meet most needs on their own.

At the organizational level, the Project could always find useful things to do. Indeed, it actively fostered family reunification (assisting individual refugees to bring family members from the region to Canada) and "responsorship" (aiding private groups that wished to bring in and resettle additional refugees from Southeast Asia). The initial rationale, however, was fading, a consequence of the movement's own success. In May, the furniture depot was closed due to a lack of demand, and soon after steps were taken to place the clothing depot—which had outfitted more than 2,600 new arrivals by March 1980—on a stand-alone basis, to be run by a community board rather than by the organization. The Board asked a local academic who had followed the evolution of Project 4000 since its inception, Alan Clarke of Algonquin College, to examine the implications of the organization winding up operations. Professor Clarke's chief recommendation, delivered to the board in November 1980, was "that all Project 4000 activities be concluded before December 31, 1980 except for [certain specific] financial functions..."[14] The board accepted the recommendation and Project 4000 began to consider how to phase itself out.

A young family.
Courtesy, Ron Poling/Ottawa Citizen. Reprinted by permission.

That any organization should actively plan its own demise is sufficiently unusual as to warrant examination. The central factor that made it possible was voluntarism. Project 4000 was established, operated and directed by people who had come forward out of a genuine desire to help and who never lost sight of the main goal. As Barb Gamble put it, "No one saw Project 4000 as a permanent organization. Once the aims for which it had been created had been achieved, [the organizers] were ready to move on and resume their own lives."[15]

The voluntarism of the organization was manifest in other aspects of its operations as well. Project 4000, as noted earlier, began operations with miniscule financial resources and no permanent staff. Throughout its brief life, the Project's chief strengths were the large army of enthusiastic and devoted volunteers, and the deep reserves of community support on which it was able to draw. For the entire active phase of its history, from July 1979 to the end of December 1980, Project 4000's total expenses amounted to slightly over $160,000.[16] To put this number into perspective, an internal document prepared in October 1979 — barely four months into the active phase — estimated that the financial value of the broader community contributions to refugee support had already reached $4 million,[17] twenty five times greater than Project 4000's direct expenditures to the end of 1980.

Winding down the organization brought its own set of challenges. Project 4000 had given rise to a number of innovative techniques to ease the task of resettlement, and no one wished to see them lost. The Project held consultations with OCISO and CIS to ensure that the torch was passed rather than extinguished. Witnessing the success of Project 4000's private sponsorship groups, OCISO established its Canadian Friends program, a technique to match Canadian volunteers with government-assisted refugees to provide the latter with the type of extended, informal support network that privately sponsored refugees enjoyed.[18] Other measures, from providing seed money for refugee-run enterprises in the service sector to encouraging ongoing private sponsorship groups, can be traced to the same source.

The final issue of the *Project 4000 Newsletter* appeared in January 1981. By the end of the month, the organization had closed its central office and released its small core of full-time staff. Information notices were sent to a number of individuals and organizations that had worked closely with the Project, and its files and documents were vetted and shipped to storage. Part-time secretarial assistance and telephone answering services were retained, and the City of Ottawa made office space available for such meetings as were still required. On February 19, the *Ottawa Citizen* published an open letter of appreciation from the chairman of the Project's board of directors, Romeo Maione. It read in part:

> Project 4000 was the magnificent
> and unprecedented response by the

people of the Ottawa area to the plight of the Southeast Asian refugees. The board of directors of Project 4000 would like to thank the many groups and individuals, businesses, newspapers, churches and other organizations who have helped in the resettlement of refugees.…We hope the caring community of people who responded to the challenge [issued by] Mayor Dewar on July 12, 1979, will continue to give these new Canadians their friendship and help them find their place in the work force and the social fabric of the country.[19]

The focus of activity was now on winding up the organization expeditiously and ensuring that its remaining assets were well used. Although the board would continue to meet several times a year, the detailed work fell largely to its executive committee.

Rebuilding Lives

Phyllis Hardie's comment on the work ethic of the new arrivals reflects a widely held view among sponsors. The Canadians who had direct dealings with the new arrivals came away impressed and encouraged by the refugees' determination to become self-sufficient at the earliest possible date. For many newcomers, the goal would remain beyond reach until they had acquired competence in either English or French.

Obtaining employment remained a top priority for all. Those who arrived with a grasp of one of Canada's official languages usually entered the workforce quite quickly. Even those who spoke little or no English or French often succeeded in finding jobs within a short timeframe.

An Song Hoang, a veteran of the South Vietnamese armed forces, fled Vietnam in the summer of 1980 on a small and crowded vessel. Off the coast of Thailand, pirates attacked the refugee craft. In the fighting, 30 of the 138 people aboard were killed, by their attackers or by the waters of the South China Sea. When the survivors eventually put ashore, they were immediately confined in a refugee camp. An was fortunate; a younger sister had settled in Ottawa shortly after the end of the Vietnam War and was prepared to assist him. He was quickly selected for admission to Canada.

Arriving in Ottawa in the fall of 1980, An immediately found work in a restaurant. In retrospect, he believes that he might have been wiser to have taken the full-time language training then available, but he had enough English to get by. Beyond anything else, he wanted to earn enough money to repay his sister and to bring his fiancée from Vietnam to join him. While his debt to his sister was quickly satisfied, it would be many years before An would be reunited with his fiancée. With a mother suffering from cancer and a father incarcerated as a political prisoner, she felt that she could not leave. An made the best of it, working hard and sponsoring his own parents, as well as a younger brother and his family. Finally, in 1992, 12 years after An had left Vietnam, he married his fiancée and together they moved into their own home in Ottawa. (They subsequently produced two bright and lively daughters who are now the apples of An's eye.) Over all that time, An persevered in a succession of service positions in the restaurant sector, asking little of Canadian society but the opportunity to work hard and rebuild his life.[20]

Nor was such determination limited to the world of work. Phuong Nguyen and his younger brother arrived in Ottawa in the summer of 1979 and were informally adopted by the Hughes family. Rita Hughes recalls that the town of Cumberland, on the outskirts of Ottawa, had decided to mark the International Year of the Child with a parade. She wanted to put together a float displaying the diversity of the world's children and had asked Can Le for assistance. Can had suggested that Phuong and his brother might help.

In preparation for the event, Rita invited the two boys to her

The Nguyen brothers and the Hugheses, Cumberland.
Courtesy, Phuong Nguyen.

Touring the capital.
Courtesy, Phuong Nguyen.

home. While she fully expected the association to end once the parade was over, she came home to discover the two Vietnamese boys "double riding" on bicycles with her own children and everyone having a wonderful time. As the Hugheses had an extra bedroom in their rambling old house, the two boys moved in and the Hugheses in time became their legal guardians.

Phuong, who spoke some French but very little English, enrolled that autumn in the engineering faculty of the University of Ottawa. He remembers attending his first lecture—and understanding very little of what was said. All through the fall term, he worked as hard as he could at his studies and at learning English. Christmas came and with it his first-term marks. He had failed most of his mid-year exams.

He decided that he would persevere until the end of the academic year. If his grades had not improved by then, he would drop out and look for a job. In April he received his final marks for the year—and learned that he had made the Dean's List. He pursued his studies and graduated in due course with a degree in electrical engineering.[21]

For the great majority of the new arrivals, employment was crucial, not only as a major step toward self-sufficiency, but also as a means of regaining and sustaining their own sense of self-respect and personal dignity. Most took the attitude that any job was better than no job at all. Admirable as the approach was, it came with a liability for those who arrived with professional or technical skills: few were able to find employment in their fields and were required to settle for low-paying, entry-level positions. Thus Diep Trinh, with a master's degree in business administration, found employment as a teacher of English at a local business school; his wife Tam, a former schoolteacher in Vietnam, worked as a seamstress. Few ever complained. Most were simply grateful for the opportunity to work toward self-sufficiency in the land that had given them refuge.

The biggest single hurdle the refugees faced was undoubtedly language. Without an adequate grasp of Canada's languages, many were obliged to remain within their own linguistic communities, on the margins of the wider society. In time, most of the new arrivals overcame the obstacle and began the long journey to full integration, though it required a great deal of initiative, perseverance and hard work.

PHASING OUT

Winding up Project 4000's financial responsibilities proved more complex than anticipated. As a non-profit charitable corporation, the organization was legally required either to find another body to assume its status and responsibilities or to remain in operation until all of its outstanding liabilities were satisfied and its assets disbursed. Although the operational phase of its life was over, the organization had ended 1980 with financial assets of $115,000.[22] Contributions had come in from a wide variety of individuals and institutions. Tax receipts had to be prepared and issued and, for some of the larger grants, reports compiled on how the funds had been used. Continuing to serve as intermediary between private sponsorship groups and the federal government on administrative matters remained an important task. As an additional complication, Project 4000 had itself given some financial support to a number of groups and programs over the previous 18 months. While these sums were modest, all had to be accounted for and processed. After obtaining legal advice on the alternatives open to it, the Project 4000 board decided that keeping the organization in existence for the short term was the wisest option.

The initial goal of winding up by the end of 1981 proved beyond reach. Management of the "responsorship" program, to which the Board had devoted the bulk of the remaining funds, absorbed time and energy. In addition, more than 80 private sponsorship groups remained active late in 1981—and dependent on the organization for financial reporting and tax receipt purposes. A number planned to remain operational well into 1982.

In the end, financial responsibilities continued to require attention for another 18 months. By the spring of 1983, virtually all of Project 4000's commitments had been fulfilled and most of its assets disbursed. What little remained was allocated to ongoing refugee resettlement programs—chiefly through OCISO—and the administrative costs associated with the wind up. A formal notice dated September 21, 1983, was published announcing the dissolution of the organization effective December 30, 1983.[23]

While publication of the notice signified the formal end of Project 4000, those who had been deeply engaged in making it work had marked the occasion in their own way a few weeks earlier. On September 6, a reception at Rideau Hall, the governor general's residence, honoured those who had been most directly involved. Some 200 volunteers attended, an indication of how deeply the initiative had put down roots among the people of the area.

Among those singled out for special recognition was Eleanor Ryan, an original member of the board of directors and the first and only chair of the executive committee. Eleanor had participated in the Project since its inception, had served in a variety of capacities, had deftly guided the organization through a number of delicate and potentially divisive internal management issues, and had shown herself to be tireless, effective and completely devoted to the cause of assisting the refugees. While the organization continued to enjoy widespread support until the end, it was chiefly Eleanor who resolved the many issues associated with successfully winding up the operations of a uniquely complex organization. The plaque that Eleanor received at the reception still hangs in a place of honour in her living room.

MILESTONES

The newcomers' journey toward full reconstruction and integration was neither easy nor brief. Nor did all of the refugees advance at the same pace. The goal was clear, however, and step by step they worked their way toward it. One milestone along the way was the acquisition of Canadian citizenship.

Minh Huynh arrived in Ottawa in September 1979, as one of a large family who had fled Vietnam by boat. His parents told Minh, then 13, that the family was going "on vacation," to assuage any fears the youngster might have had. Only with the passage of years did he come to understand the real nature of the risks his family had run.

Three years after they arrived in Canada, the Huynh family became eligible for citizenship. Here is how Minh describes the event:

> October 15, 1982 was a turning point for my family. On that date, the family was in our best clothes, new shoes and fully groomed. We were happy, excited and proud. That was the date that we were sworn in as Canadians, truly, proudly Canadians. Once the judge declared that we were now officially Canadians, the family all cheered, smiled, hugged and congratulated each other. We were no longer refugees....At that moment, we knew that we would have the freedom to walk, to talk, to work, to have families and to dream as Canadians. It was a good feeling, it was a tremendous feeling. It was a feeling that we will never forget.[24]

Minh stills remembers the event as a life-changing moment, on a par with getting married and welcoming the birth of his first child. Nor has he an iota of doubt about his parents' decision to risk everything in fleeing Vietnam. As he puts it, "Life is valuable but freedom is priceless."[25]

Keo Khamphoune, with her husband Bounkeo and two small children, fled Laos in 1976. After three years in a Thai refugee camp the family gained admission to Canada. Keo recalls the ceremony at which she acquired her Canadian citizenship as a very powerful and moving experience. She remembers thinking as she swore her oath, "Now we are free. Now we belong to this country!"[26]

Inevitably, some met with pitfalls and detours. Because of the marginal nature of much of their employment, the newcomers were disproportionately affected by economic downturns. As the first visible minority community of any size in the capital area, the Southeast Asians served as a lightning rod for occasional flashes of racism and discrimination. Moreover, family structures and relationships were subjected to new and sometimes intense

Now we are Canadians!
Courtesy, Diep Trinh.

pressures as individuals sought to cope with their separation from their native lands, the loss of family members dead or dispersed in the exodus, and the impact of North American culture and values on traditional relationships and behaviour.

Despite the challenges and difficulties, the newcomers worked hard at whatever employment they were able to secure, pooled their resources and re-established a sense of community. Some were soon helping others less fortunate than themselves.

Within a few months of the Trinhs' arrival, Diep was already volunteering several hours a week at a downtown centre that helped newcomers find their way around. He recalls the growing satisfaction he derived over the years from teaching English to other new arrivals. While the position was never very well remunerated, he found it deeply rewarding to assist his students, coaching them on the questions they should expect during a job interview and transporting them to possible job openings.

Diep stressed two basic rules to his students: never be late for an interview and master the English language. He remembers wryly one episode when both of his rules went out the window. He was using his old car to transport three of his students—a Nicaraguan, a Laotian and a Hungarian—to apply for positions at a large truck repair garage. It was raining heavily and partway there, the engine died. "You are all mechanics," he said. "Fix my car." The three students got out into the pelting rain, lifted the hood, and began poking and probing. A running consultation took place in a unique mixture of English, Spanish, Laotian and Hungarian. Finally, one of the three put his head in through the window. "Check the gas gauge," he said. Sure enough, the car had simply run out of gas.

Arriving late for the job interview, Diep apologized profusely to the garage manager, insisting that the fault was entirely his and that his students should not suffer for his mistake. The manager eventually agreed to interview all three. Diep was certain that the one person who would *not* be hired was the Hungarian; even though he had the most experience, his English was by far the weakest. Interviews over, the manger re-emerged and offered a position—to the Hungarian!

In the car on the way home, Diep asked his student how he had managed to do it. "Easy," came the reply. "Another Hungarian mechanic already works there and he translated for me."[27]

Other newcomers followed a path similar to Diep's, preferring personal fulfillment to material gain. After graduation, Phuong Nguyen secured employment as an electrical engineer in the burgeoning high-tech sector, and soon won promotion and recognition for his skills. After some years he decided that he wanted to be more directly involved with people, particularly those in need. He currently works for the municipality as a counsellor in the field of social assistance and provides translation services to various judicial and administrative bodies when the need arises.

For most of the newcomers, securing educational opportunities for their children was another important marker in the reconstruction process. In discussing the reasons that prompted them to leave their homelands, the refugees consistently cited concern about their children's future as a major motive. Some who might have been prepared to live with persecution and marginalization themselves could not endure the prospect of their children being consigned to the same fate. For the newcomers, seeing their children do well in school validated their decision to flee and provided hope that life in Canada would provide a brighter future, if not immediately for themselves, then eventually and indirectly through their children.

The children certainly heeded the lesson. They adapted quickly and easily to the Canadian educational system, worked hard and frequently headed their classes in terms of academic achievement. Their Canadian teachers remember them with affection and respect. With the passage of time, a large number secured post-secondary education, and many have gone on to earn advanced degrees and professional certification. For many of the older generation, perhaps hampered by lingering linguistic difficulties, the clear and demonstrable success of their offspring has been a continuing source of satisfaction.

Each person's story is unique: each person's story is universal. Katherine Van Nguyen arrived in Canada in 1980, with her husband and a year old child, under the provisions of Québec's refugee assistance program. Life was difficult at first as the couple adapted to the demands of a different culture, Canadian winters, and separation from everything they had known. They persevered and gradually rebuilt their lives. After seven years in Montréal and two more children, the family moved to Ottawa and the reconstruction process began once again. Although the Van Nguyens prospered, tragedy struck when Katherine's husband died prematurely, leaving her to raise her three young sons on her own. Despite the obstacles, she saw to it that all three boys obtained a post-secondary education. Her pride in their achievements—notably "her baby's" selection by his university to represent it at an international competition in Thailand—shines through as she recounts the triumphs and the trials of her life.[28]

For some, the long journey led to destinations little short of miraculous. Huot Tea came to Canada in February 1979 sponsored by Archbishop J.A. Plourde, head of the Catholic archdiocese of Ottawa. Huot, then 17, had been orphaned in the Cambodian genocide. His original family had consisted of his parents, a brother and three sisters. He knew that his mother and father, his brother and one sister had died and he had lost all contact with any other surviving family members. He settled into his new life in Canada, earned a degree from the University of Ottawa, pursued further training in computer studies, married and made a place for himself in his adopted country. In 2000, a friend in Montréal told him that he planned to revisit Cambodia. Huot gave him a picture and asked him to put a notice in the paper on the off chance that a relative might see it. Within days, the friend was contacted by a woman who identified herself as Huot's aunt. She said that two of his sisters had survived and were living in Montréal and Toronto. Two decades after their family had been shattered, Huot and his two sisters were reunited. Both sisters have children of their own and the three families now get together regularly.[29]

Huot Tea and Archbishop J.A. Plourde.
Courtesy, Huot Tea.

Looking Back

For those who participated, residents and newcomers alike, Project 4000 was a luminous moment, a chapter in their lives that continues to glow despite the passage of years. Sponsors recall the time as one of invitation: to dig down deep and discover what they truly believed in; to act on those beliefs, not in mock-heroic fashion but in the day-to-day events of their lives; to encounter and embrace strangers in need; and, ultimately, to learn that they were no strangers at all. For Pat Marshall, "It was something of a golden era. People acted out of a sense of genuine compassion. It was a time when the claims of strangers were heard with sympathy and respect."[30] A recurring theme among sponsors is that the satisfaction they derived from their actions on behalf of the newcomers far outweighed any costs they assumed. Peter Wiebe of the Ottawa Mennonite Church recalls:

> The youngest in the first family [the OMC sponsored] was only eight to 10 years of age…very shy and reticent. Years later, I was riding the city bus back to my home after work …when suddenly this person snuggled up to me on the seat with a huge smile on her face. To my surprise and delight it was this girl, now a young lady, who was just ever so delighted to see me, as I her. She was bubbly and talkative. That expressed her appreciation for our efforts more than words could.[31]

The former refugees are equally passionate. The decision to flee was extremely difficult, a desperate gamble in which they staked their lives and often those of their children on a faint and distant hope. Resettlement in Canada came at a price, and for those who could not adapt, it was sometimes high. That said, a deep and abiding conviction that they made the right choice permeates the comments of the Southeast Asians. Nor is it only the security and success that they and their families now enjoy that sustains this conviction. Out of the sponsor-refugee relationship were born ties that endure to this day. That the younger members of the family the Pikes helped to sponsor still refer to them as "Aunt Sue and Uncle George" and Phuong Nguyen still addresses Rita Hughes as "Mom" says as much as needs be said.

Equally strong among the newcomers is a profound sense of gratitude for the actions of Canada and Canadians in providing them with an opportunity to rebuild their lives. As they look back on their own personal achievements, witness their children moving steadily and successfully into mainstream Canadian life, and reflect on the deep roots they have put down in the Ottawa area, the former refugees are among this country's proudest citizens.

One small vignette perhaps best illustrates the point. A few years ago, Chamroeun Lay took his two Canadian-born teenage children back to Cambodia. The visit meant a great deal to him, as he was able to locate friends and family members whom he hadn't seen in decades. The youngsters, though amazed at how hard people their age had to work just to survive, also benefited from the experience. The contrast between their own comfortable lives in Canada and the realities that young Cambodians faced daily brought home to them how much they had taken for granted. And yet, the longer Chamroeun stayed, the deeper grew the feeling that he no longer belonged, that he was a stranger in the land of his birth. Everything had changed so much since his departure in the mid-1970s.

As their plane touched down in Vancouver on their way back to Ottawa, Chamroeun remembers saying to himself, "I'm home now."[32]

Results

During its brief existence, Project 4000 stimulated and channelled the humanitarian impulses of the Ottawa area, drew in hundreds of volunteers to make the organization work, and encouraged and supported thousands of private sponsors in their efforts to welcome Southeast Asian refugees and help them rebuild their lives. In the end, what did Marion Dewar's initiative accomplish? As it turns out, a great deal.

At the most tangible level, Project 4000 was instrumental in resettling several thousand new Canadians in the Ottawa region. By October 1983, the Project had "assisted private groups to bring in what is now close to 2000 refugees. A further 1638 arrived under Government sponsorship."[33] Beyond the 3,600 who arrived during the life of the Project, many hundreds more would come in the months and years ahead, as the early arrivals began to reunite their sundered families and as Ottawa's reputation as a positive environment for resettlement and reconstruction spread.

The region was deeply affected by the Project. People from all walks of life came together to work for a common goal. Neighbours who had barely known each other well enough to exchange greetings on the street found themselves caught up in a shared undertaking to welcome strangers to their communities. Social solidarity reached levels rarely seen in peacetime. It faded somewhat with the passage of time, but its benefits have endured. In Archbishop Plourde's assessment, the initiative contributed strongly and directly to better relations among the various faith-based communities of the region by bringing them together in pursuit of a shared objective. Almost 30 years later, he believes that interfaith relations continue to reap the rewards. Moreover, the newcomers had a major impact. While their numbers were not huge, they were large enough to diversify the demographic composition of the region, expand its economic base, add strong new Asian cultural elements and, in the Archbishop's words, "change the way people in Ottawa looked at the world and at other people."[34]

While there may well have been costs associated with Project 4000, three decades later they are indiscernible. From today's perspective, the most striking feature of the objections raised at the time is simply how profoundly wrong they were. The region was not inundated by foreigners; Canadian workers did not lose out to the newcomers; and the quality of life in the neighbourhoods in which the refugees settled went up—not down. If ever a persuasive case were needed to illustrate the adage of "doing well by doing good," Project 4000 and its continuing influence on the Ottawa area certainly provide it.

Elliot Tepper, an Asian studies specialist at Carleton University, responded to the crisis by encouraging fellow academics in the Canadian Asian Studies Association to produce a book that Project 4000 sponsors and others could use to deepen their understanding of Southeast Asian cultures and practices. Looking back at the national and local responses to the humanitarian emergency from today's vantage point, he sees in them much of enduring value. "The Southeast Asian refugee crisis," he states, "brought out the very best in our national character. We dug down deep and found rich resources on which to draw. The net result was an outstanding success for Canada. While we certainly did good to the newcomers arriving in our communities, we ourselves were the primary beneficiaries."[35]

Nor was Project 4000's influence limited to the federal capital region. Flora MacDonald has described how the initiative strengthened the hand of those who wanted Canada to take a leadership role in dealing with the refugee crisis. The Project also had a major impact on the grassroots responses of Canadians across the country. Marion Dewar's challenge to other cities to take action was widely reported, and the establishment of Project 4000 attracted national media attention. Mike Molloy, head of the federal immigration authorities' Refugee Task Force, was a key figure in developing and managing Canada's national response to the crisis.

"There is no question," he writes, "that Project 4000 in Ottawa and Operation Lifeline in Toronto were the most influential of the local initiatives responding to the 'Boat People' crisis. Project 4000 galvanized a very large sector of the Ottawa-based public service, brought influential religious leaders…squarely on board and, most importantly, established the precedent of municipal leaders taking a strong role in mobilizing their communities."

He continues, "The powerful leadership exercised by Marion Dewar in particular, and the public's tremendous response to that leadership, were highly visible to members of the Clark government and to parliamentarians generally and confirmed that a strong Canadian commitment to the resettlement of Indochinese refugees would enjoy active support from Canadians in general and their local leaders."[36]

Finally, Canada learned a great deal from the massive involvement of private citizens in welcoming, resettling and integrating newcomers. A number of innovative techniques and approaches that have found their way into general practice had their genesis in Project 4000. Equally important, immigration pitfalls and obstacles that might never have occurred to native-born Canadians were identified and creative means found, if not to resolve them, at least to begin the process. The experiences of the newcomers in Ottawa and across Canada eased the way for the tens of thousands from other parts of the world who have come after them.

Shortly after Marion Dewar launched the idea of Ottawans organizing to give effective assistance to the refugees from Vietnam, Cambodia and Laos, a reporter asked her why she was risking her career in this manner. From a domestic political perspective, the mayor had much to lose and nothing very evident to gain. "For Dewar," he wrote, "the move is obviously a political gamble. If it fails, [she said,] 'I'll fall flat on my face.' If it works, she will have given the city something to be proud of."[37] By any standard, Marion Dewar's initiative was, and remains, a gift that keeps on giving. In the unfolding story of Ottawa and Canada, Project 4000 remains a luminous and inspiring chapter: a convincing demonstration of the ability of ordinary people to accomplish deeds both great and good.

CHAPTER 5

EPILOGUE

What wisdom can you find that is greater than kindness?

—Jean Jacques Rousseau

POINTS OF REFERENCE

In 1982, the federal authorities funded a study of conditions among the Southeast Asian refugees in the capital region. Led by an academic psychiatrist at the University of Ottawa, the analysts cast their central concern in the following terms:

> The Canadian response to the plight of the Southeast Asian refugees during the recent years has once more upheld our humanitarian tradition of providing a safe haven to the displaced and the persecuted.... For the country, it has been an exciting time and a rewarding experience. As for the refugees, they are deeply grateful to Canada for allowing them the opportunity for a new life.
>
> But how well are our refugees doing?[1]

An extensive questionnaire was designed and translated into Vietnamese, Chinese, Cambodian and Laotian to gather information on a large representative sample of the newcomers. Native speakers were hired in the fall of 1982 to conduct interviews in the mother tongues of the refugees. At the time, the overall size of the community[2] was approximately 4,100, of whom 80 percent had been in Canada for less than three years. Some 89 percent lived on the Ontario side of the Ottawa River—overwhelmingly in the City of Ottawa—and the remaining 11 percent in the Québec portion of the capital region. The findings offer a fine-grained picture of the newcomers during their early years in the area, and a coherent set of reference points against which to assess subsequent developments.

The overall picture was decidedly mixed. As a group, the newcomers clearly faced significant challenges. Unemployment rates were very high, over three times higher than that of the population at large. Privately sponsored refugees fared better than the government-assisted newcomers, but the former's unemployment rate was still twice as high as the regional average. Among those who had found jobs, the great majority were working in unskilled or semi-skilled positions in the service sector, or in the garment and electronic industries. Even those with high skill levels or professional credentials faced an uphill struggle; less than 10 percent were working in positions commensurate with their qualifications. As to the refugees as a whole, the great majority were poor, with 80 percent of the households surveyed living below Canada's poverty line. Virtually the entire community lived in rental accommodation, with fewer than 2 percent owning their own homes.

Official language skills, the key means to interaction with the wider Canadian society, were still rudimentary. While nearly all had learned some English or French, for most people it was minimal. Almost three quarters reported that they understood less than half of the English spoken in conversation and over eight in 10 had great difficulty expressing themselves in English. Among heads of households, only 15 percent assessed their skills as adequate to hold down a job requiring English and less than 30 percent thought that they had enough English to "get by in everyday life."

Beyond these objective conditions, most of the refugees were still struggling to deal with the trauma of their past. Almost all had had to deal with family dislocation. Over 90 percent reported that members of their families were still missing. In addition, the changing roles of spouses, shifts in relationships between the young and the old, and huge differences between the cultures of Southeast Asia and of Canada—and North America—all created additional stresses. In the circumstances, it was hardly surprising that strong majorities reported suffering from homesickness, worries about the future and loneliness. "It would appear," commented the analysts "...those symptoms are indicators of a high prevalence of depression and anxiety among the refugee population."[3]

However, the picture also contained many positive elements. As a group, the refugees brought with them a strong work ethic, an abiding sense of appreciation for the opportunities that Canada's peace and freedom provided, and an iron-clad determination to rebuild their lives. In addition, youth, physical health, an entrepreneurial spirit, respect for learning, patience, self-denial, and strong family and social bonds all constituted important assets as the community embarked on its course to join mainstream Canadian society.

The refugees also possessed another, perhaps even more important, quality: a realization that they had already met and overcome threats far more lethal than any they were likely to meet in their new homeland. For people who had survived a typhoon in a small craft at sea, crept through an unmarked Cambodian minefield or dealt with a pack of human predators on the Laotian-Thai border, the obstacles to rebuilding their lives in Canada—while serious—could hardly seem insurmountable. Perhaps it was for that reason that even though the great majority lived below the poverty line in 1982, few considered themselves impoverished.[4]

Summing up the attitude of the newcomers as the journey toward integration began in earnest, the survey reported that "...the Southeast Asian refugees are highly motivated to learn and to adapt to their new environment. They are eager to achieve self-sufficiency and to become good citizens."[5]

Steps on a Journey

The intervening years have witnessed an impressive rate of progress by the former refugees, as individuals and as a community. Political integration occurred very quickly. Virtually all became citizens of their new country as soon as Canadian law allowed. Some made it a point to apply for citizenship on the very first day they became eligible to do so. Within a few years, the new arrivals were refugees no longer, having become new Canadians with the same rights and obligations as any other citizen.

Economic and social integration were necessarily more complex. Because of the newcomers' initial concentration in entry-level jobs, they tended to suffer disproportionately in periods of economic recession. "Last in, first out" was a common experience. Layoffs in the

New Canadians.
Courtesy, Lê-Phan, Vietnamese Canadian Centre

Ottawa-area high-tech sector, a major source of their employment in the 1980s and 1990s, hit the new arrivals particularly hard. Toronto, Vancouver and Montréal, with their more diversified economies and larger Southeast Asian populations, proved continuing sources of attraction, offering opportunity to some but probably slowing the community's growth in the capital region.

Despite the challenges, the Southeast Asians as a group flourished. A Vietnamese proverb has it that "perseverance turns iron into gold." The new land offered many opportunities, but none came on platters of silver—or gold. Above all, the values the newcomers brought with them were the key element that allowed them to surmount the obstacles they faced. Steadily and without drama, the former refugees moved ahead. One former refugee, long active in the Vietnamese community, described the steps on the journey in the following terms:

> For the first three to five years after arrival, most people concentrated on becoming self-sufficient and did so by finding permanent employment and becoming familiar with the Canadian way of doing things. After 10 years or so, many had established their own small businesses. By 15 to 20 years after arrival, their children had often secured a higher education and the parents had acquired their own homes.[6]

By the time the national census of 2001 was carried out, the evidence of significant progress was unmistakable. The newcomers' overall situation, in absolute terms, had improved sharply. Even more striking were the advances they had made relative to long-established residents. While gaps remained, the newcomers had "caught up" substantially. The improvement was all the more notable because of the general growth in numbers, wealth, and educational levels that Canada and the national capital area had experienced. For the newcomers to move toward general parity with the local population implied a fast relative rate of progress, as the targets themselves were moving quickly ahead.

The census revealed that the community as a whole had more than doubled since 1982, to almost 8,700 people.[7] Relative to the wider regional population, its position had changed less radically, as the Ottawa-Hull metropolitan area had also grown by almost 50 percent. Nonetheless, the increase in the number of residents with Vietnamese, Cambodian and Laotian origins, in absolute and relative terms, spoke to deepening roots and a blossoming presence.

Within the regional economy, the participation rates of the former refugees—the proportions of working-age individuals seeking or engaged in active work—were within a few percentage points of that of the broader "Canadian" population, although unemployment rates remained sharply higher. The newcomers had moved well beyond the entry-level occupations that had once sustained them, diversifying and expanding their employment skills. Across the full occupational spectrum, people of Southeast Asian extraction were active in increasing numbers, as they were in the broader Canadian economy.[8]

Employment earnings reflected the former refugees' growing economic role. By 2001, the Southeast Asians as a group were earning almost 85 percent of the average employment earnings of the wider native-born population. Important gaps remained. The communities did not all move forward at the same rate and the incidence of low incomes among those of Southeast Asian origin remained much higher than in the population at large. Nonetheless, relative to the days when 80 percent of their numbers had lived below the poverty line, the new Canadians had clearly achieved a great deal.[9]

Census data on educational levels reflected the same pattern of steady, broad-based progress. By 2001, the community had closed much of the gap in formal educational levels with the native-born population. Indeed, the percentage of Southeast Asians who held completed university degrees slightly exceeded the level among residents of "Canadian" origin.[10] The indicators of further progress were excellent. In the key age group of 15 to 24 years, the percentage of Southeast Asian youth in full-time attendance at school was significantly higher than it was for the population at large.[11]

In short, looking back at the accomplishments of the previous two decades, the former refugees had many reasons to feel both pride and gratitude. While challenges still lay ahead, the most serious had been met and overcome. New Canadians of Vietnamese, Cambodian and Laotian origin were leaving the margins and moving steadily toward the centre, and there was every reason to believe that they would continue to do so. The conditions of 1982 had been transformed.

Just fine, thank you.
Courtesy, Quy Luong, Vietnamese Canadian Centre

The 25th Anniversary Celebrations

In 2004, the Vietnamese Canadian Federation marked the 25th anniversary of Project 4000 by organizing an extensive photo exhibition of the travails of the boat people. Fittingly, the exhibit opened on Remembrance Day, November 11, and ran for three weeks. In conjunction with the event, the Federation also organized a reunion dinner on November 20 for former refugees, sponsors, friends and volunteers.

The exhibit attracted widespread media coverage and a large number of visitors. Viewing the stark, powerful images of the refugees' flight to freedom proved a moving and emotional experience. Many former refugees made a point of visiting the display with their children so that the next generation could begin to understand the sufferings of its parents and grandparents—and the courage and endurance with which they had borne them.

Flora MacDonald, Marion Dewar and organizers.
Courtesy, Lê-Phan, Vietnamese Canadian Centre

The anniversary celebrations summoned up a wide range of reactions and emotions among former refugees and ex-sponsors alike. Sorrow, gratitude, pride, determination, affection, humour, respect and humility—all were present. For former refugees, it was impossible to recall the events of 25 years earlier without profound sorrow over the decades of war and suffering that their former homelands had undergone, and the very large number of people who had died while trying to escape. Equally evident was a deep sense of gratitude for having survived and having being given a second chance. While Canada had offered a haven, the newcomers too had worked diligently and patiently to become good citizens and to contribute to their new country. The sentiments of the former refugees were eloquently captured in an address at the exhibition by one former "boat person," Huong Nguyen:

> Many of us here have relatives and friends who departed Vietnam but who never made it, and our hearts ache when we think of them.…We are the lucky ones who made it. And we made it to Canada thanks to the generosity of the Canadian people, of the private sponsors who put up money and opened their

When a few good people unite…
Courtesy, Lê-Phan, Vietnamese Canadian Centre

hearts and their homes to take us in.…There are doctors, pharmacists, dentists, oncologists, surgeons, professors, teachers, lawyers, engineers, technicians and other service providers who are Vietnamese boat people or children of Vietnamese boat people.…We are happy that we have the opportunity to pay back the community that has opened its arms to us, and we are happy to serve all the people in this community.[12]

Former sponsors were equally moved. For many, Project 4000 had been a unique opportunity to act on their own core values. As their dealings with the newcomers increased, so did the sponsors' respect and affection for "their refugees." The personal qualities of the newcomers—their self-discipline, patience, adaptability and determination—moved their relationships beyond the two-dimensional dynamic of giver and receiver of aid. Close friendships developed that endured through the years. Routine daily events that at one time had baffled sponsor or refugee became rich sources of amusement and shared memories with the passage

Marion Dewar receiving an award.
Courtesy, Lê-Phan, Vietnamese Canadian Centre

of time. With the sponsors' greater knowledge of the newcomers and their experiences came, as well, a deeper sense of the many blessings Canadians enjoy and the power ordinary citizens possess when they share a common goal. As Marion Dewar put it:

> [Project 4000] was the people's finest moment, not mine. All I did was direct the traffic. Ottawa is today a better city because of Project 4000. It made us conscious of occurrences in the world where our fellow human beings were dying and we did something about it. But the greatest part of this story is that the country came together. It was the grassroots that came together and showed the power of what a few people could do.[13]

PASSING THE TORCH

Since the 25th anniversary of Project 4000, the general current of the former refugees' steady progress and integration into the Canadian mainstream has strengthened and deepened. A few numbers drawn from a recent survey by the Vietnamese community on the socio-economic integration of its members, contrasted against the conditions of 1982, illustrate just how far the former refugees have come. In 2004–05, one third of the capital area's Vietnamese community was Canadian born. Virtually all community members— 97 percent—had become Canadian citizens. Knowledge of Canada's official languages was up sharply, with 82 percent reporting an extensive or adequate grasp of English and 34 percent an equivalent command of French. On housing, over 73 percent of the respondents owned their own home or apartment. Moreover, attachment to the new homeland was extremely strong, with 88 percent indicating that life in Canada was much better or somewhat better than it had been in Vietnam.[14] While information on the Cambodian and Laotian

Enriching Ottawa's cultural traditions.
Courtesy, Quy Luong, Vietnamese Canadian Centre

The rising generation.
Courtesy, Khoi Nguyen, Vietnamese Canadian Centre

communities is more anecdotal, it points in the same general direction.

In short, the core ethnic communities are flourishing economically and socially. Their children pursue higher education in large numbers and maintain a high standard of academic achievement. The younger generation is moving steadily to assume its rightful place in Canadian society, and to contribute to that society.

Moreover, today's community leaders, through such initiatives as a national youth leadership workshop organized by the Vietnamese Canadian Federation in the spring of 2007, are seeing to it that the hard-won lessons of the past are not forgotten.

New issues and challenges may emerge in due course. While full economic parity with the broader Canadian population is closer than ever for the former refugees, some gaps in some areas may persist. Members of the younger generation in time may come to feel a need to balance and integrate their Canadian nationality with their Southeast Asian cultural traditions. Given the scope and number of obstacles already met and

The standard bearers.
Courtesy, Quy Luong, Vietnamese Canadian Centre

overcome, the constituent communities will undoubtedly meet any new challenge successfully—and Canada and the capital region will be all the better for it.

The encounter of courage and compassion may, "if will and grace are joined," bring forth gifts of abiding value. In the summer of 1980, confined in a Thai refugee camp, An Song Hoang learned that he had been accepted for admission to Canada. He began to compose a song addressed to his new homeland that over the years became his personal testament. In the trials and the triumphs, the losses and the blessings that An experienced can be glimpsed the lives of hundreds of thousands of others, each unique, each sharing a common destiny. An Song Hoang's greeting to his new country seems a fitting note on which to conclude this work.

CHÀO CANADA

Tác giả: Hoàng Song An

Chào mừng Canada
Chào mừng Canada
Xứ yên lành, lớn vô cùng,
Nhìn quê người mà xót quê hương …

Chào mừng Canada
Chào mừng Canada
Nắng êm đềm, Tuyết chan hòa
Nhìn quê người mà nhớ quê hương …

Biển đông xanh bao la,
Thuyền ra khơi phong ba,
Cứ đi liều,
Cuối chân trời
Gặp phái đoàn Canada

Người Canada vui tươi
Tình Canada như hoa
Đón dân mình, rất chân tình,
Nghe trong lòng bao nỗi xót xa …

Điệp khúc: Đến hôm nay xa quê hương bao xuân qua
                Vẫn luôn luôn mang trong tim hoài cố hương
                Dòng Rồng-Tiên
                Việt nam tôi,
                Xin có đôi lời biết ơn
                Dòng Rồng-Tiên
                Việt nam tôi,
                Xin có đôi lời biết ơn …

GREETINGS CANADA

An Song Hoang

Greetings to Canada
Greetings to Canada
A country peaceful and immense
Seeing your homeland, I feel sorry for mine …

Greetings to Canada
Greetings to Canada
With gentle sunshine and overflowing snow
Seeing your homeland, I lament for mine …

To the boundless blue open sea of the East
My boat headed out against storm and wave
Accepting the risk of leaving my home
Canada's delegate I met
On the far horizon.

Canadians are light-hearted
Like flowers, do Canadians love
My countrymen are sincerely welcome here
Yet still do I feel in many ways tormented …

Refrain: Away from my homeland for many springs
Still am I always homesick.
From my Vietnamese ancestry of Dragon and Angel
I offer my gratitude
From my Vietnamese ancestry of Dragon and Angel
I offer my gratitude …

CHAPTER NOTES

CHAPTER 1 NOTES

No citations.

CHAPTER 2 NOTES

1. Even today, estimates of casualties sustained during the Vietnam War remain highly uncertain and often politicized. American sources tend to place the toll at the lower end of the range, while official Vietnamese estimates are consistently much higher. The range cited in the text has been extrapolated from a number of standard references, including the *Encyclopaedia Britannica*, the *Funk and Wagnalls New World Encyclopedia* and Wikipedia (online).

2. R.J. Rummel, Chapter 4, "Statistics of Cambodian Democide," p. 1, in *Statistics of Democide: Genocide and Mass Murder Since 1900*.

3. UNHCR, Chapter 4, "Flight from Indochina," in *The State of the World's Refugees—2000*, p.81.

4. UNHCR, "Flight from Indochina", p.81.

5. *Ibid.*, p. 82.

6. CBC, "Re-education camps…or death camps?"

7. Lawrence Lam, *From Being Uprooted to Surviving*, p. 2.

8. UNHCR, "Flight from Indochina," p. 82.

9. Bruce Grant, *The Boat People: An Age Investigation*, p.80, put the number of Vietnamese who had fled by boat between May,1975 and mid-1979 at 292,000.

10. Ian Hamilton [personal interview], May 22, 2007.

11. Stephen Blizzard [personal interview], May 22, 2007.

12. W.C. Robinson, *Terms of Refuge*, p. 138.

13. CBC, "Pirates and sinking ships: One refugee's story."

14. UNHCR, "Flight from Indochina," p. 92.

15. G.S. Goodwin-Gill, as quoted in Grant, *The Boat People*, p. 205.

16. Employment and Immigration Canada, *Indochinese Refugees: The Canadian Response, 1979 and 1980*, tables, pp. 20–27.

17. CBC, "Refuge for the Unwanted."

18. Bruce Grant, *The Boat People*, p. 79.

19. Ian Hamilton [personal interview], May 22, 2007.

20. As quoted in Bruce Grant, *The Boat People*, p. 80.

21. As quoted in Bruce Grant, *The Boat People*, p. 158.

22. UNHCR, "Flight from Indochina," p. 83.

23. *Ibid.*, p. 103.

CHAPTER 3 NOTES

1. EIC, *Indochinese Refugees: The Canadian Response, 1979 and 1980*, p. 33.

2. Howard Adelman, *Canada and the Indochinese Refugees*, p. 2. Adelman wrote of the 1979–80 period: "None of the [public opinion] polls indicated that a majority of Canadians were ever in favour of increasing the Indochinese intake (not even at the time of intensive media coverage of the refugees' sufferings, when the intake figure was only 8,000)."

3. "Canada to take more refugees", *Globe & Mail*. The increase from 7,000 to 8,000 was announced on June 21, 1979. An additional 4,000 refugees were expected to enter Canada under private sponsorship auspices.

4. Flora MacDonald [personal interview], June 28, 2007.

5. "Southeast Asians," *The Canadian Encyclopedia* [online].

6. For a more detailed discussion, see Howard Adelman, *op. cit.*, p. 139.

7. Much of the information in this section was provided by Marion Dewar [personal interview], May 14, 2007.

8. Can Le [personal interview], June 19, 2007.

9. Phil Kinsman, "'Boat People' capture hearts of Ottawans" *Ottawa Citizen*.

10. Russ Mills [personal interview], May 15, 2007.

11. Richard Hardy [personal interview], July 16, 2007.

12. Alan Breakspear [personal interview], October 26, 2007.

13. Russ Mills [personal interview], May 15, 2007.

14. Russ Mills, "Helping you to help others", *Ottawa Citizen*.

15. Barb and Dan Gamble [personal interview], June 27, 2007.

16. Sue and George Pike [personal interview], June 28, 2007.

17. Anne McIntyre, "City rallies to refugee aid", *Ottawa Journal*.

18. Don Gerber [personal communication], July 4, 2007.

19. Project 4000 Record, Application for Incorporation of a Corporation Without Share Capital, July 18, 1979 [Eleanor Ryan papers].

20. Project 4000 Record, Minutes of the Meeting of the Board of Directors of Project 4000, August 2, 1979 [Eleanor Ryan papers].

21. Barb and Dan Gamble [personal interview], June 27, 2007.

CHAPTER 4 NOTES

1. Sue and George Pike [personal interview], June 28, 2007.

2. Chamroeun Lay [personal interview], August 29, 2007.

3. Project 4000 Record, Attachment to the Minutes of the 10th Meeting of the Board of Directors, December 13, 1979; Letter covering a Grant Application to the Department of the Secretary of State [Eleanor Ryan papers].

4. Robert Bailey [personal interview], November 29, 2007.

5. According to the EIC's *Indochinese Refugees: The Canadian Response, 1979 and 1980*, [table, p.29] at the end of 1980, there were 7,675 private sponsorship groups across Canada, or approximately one for every 3,100 Canadians. With 379 groups and a population base of 718,000, the Ottawa-Hull census metropolitan area had a ratio of one group for every 1,900 residents.

6. Tony Enns [personal communication], October 7, 2007.

7. Pat Marshall [personal interview], August 22, 2007.

8. Project 4000 Record, Eleanor Ryan to Claire Lapointe (Department of the Secretary of State), November 17, 1981 [Eleanor Ryan papers].

9. Diep Trinh [personal interview], September 4, 2007.

10. Elizabeth Rapley [personal interview], October 2, 2007.

11. Liem Duong [personal interview], October 10, 2007.

12. Phyllis Hardie [personal interview], September 6, 2007.

13. Nancy and Doug Umbach [personal interview], September 28, 2007.

14. A. Clarke, Project 4000: Final Report to the Board of Directors, November 1980, p.3. [Eleanor Ryan papers].

15. Barb and Dan Gamble [personal interview], June 27, 2007.

16. Project 4000 Record, Attachment, Auditors' Report and Financial Statements, to Eleanor Ryan to Claire Lapointe, *op. cit.* [Eleanor Ryan papers].

17. Project 4000 Record, Attachment, Proposals for the Future Operations of Project 4000 and Budget Requirements, to Minutes of the 7th Meeting of the Board of Directors, September 23, 1979 [Eleanor Ryan papers].

18. Pat Marshall, *op. cit.*, recalls the success of the program as such that it was later adopted as a model by federal resettlement officials and extended across the country as the Host Program.

19. Romeo Maione, "Keep caring", *Ottawa Citizen*.

20. An Song Hoang [personal interview], October 4, 2007.

21. Rita Hughes and Phuong Nguyen [personal interview], September 18, 2007.

22. Project 4000 Record, Auditors' Report and Financial Statements, *op. cit.* [Eleanor Ryan papers].

23. *Ottawa Citizen*, September 24, 1983, p.99. The three-month notice period was required to ensure that all outstanding obligations had been met.

24. Minh Huynh [statement at the 25th anniversary of Project 4000], November 2004.

25. Minh Huynh [personal interview], October 19, 2007.

26. Bounkeo and Keo Khamphoune [personal interview], September 17, 2007.

27. Diep Trinh, *op. cit.*

28. Katherine Van Nguyen [personal interview], October 13, 2007.

29. Huot Tea [personal interview], October 9, 2007.

30. Pat Marshall, *op. cit.*

31. Peter Wiebe and Tony Enns [personal communication], October 9, 2007.

32. Chamroeun Lay, *op. cit.*

33. Project 4000 Record, Appendix B to Minutes of the 27th Meeting of the Board of Directors, October 27, 1983 [Eleanor Ryan papers]. Although the Clark government initially promised to match the number of privately sponsored refugees on a one-for-one basis, the private response was so strong that the government soon faced the choice of abandoning the formula or again raising the overall intake target. By December 1979, the number of privately sponsored refugees had already reached 26,000 and voices within government were questioning the wisdom of exceeding the 50,000 overall target announced in July. After consulting with a number of refugee relief organizations, the government dropped the matching formula. (For details, see "Minutes of the 10th Meeting of the Board of Directors," December 13, 1979.)

34. J.A. Plourde [personal interview], September 12, 2007.

35. Elliot Tepper [personal interview], October 16, 2007. The work is *Southeast Asian Exodus: From Tradition to Resettlement* (see bibliography).

36. Mike Molloy [personal communication], September 20, 2007.

37. Phil Kinsman, "'Boat people' capture hearts of Ottawans" *Ottawa Citizen*.

CHAPTER 5 NOTES

1. S.D. Nguyen, T. Cooke and T.Q. Phung, *Ottawa-Carleton Southeast Asian Refugees: Needs Assessment*, p.49. Although the term "Southeast Asian" clearly covers a much wider range of peoples and states, in the study it refers exclusively to the countries and former residents of Vietnam, Cambodia and Laos. The same practice has been followed in this chapter, chiefly to avoid excessive repetition.

2. *Ibid.*, p. 6. The total number consisted of 300 Laotians, 800 Cambodians, 1,200 Vietnamese and 1,800 Chinese/Vietnamese.

3. *Ibid.*, p. 19.

4. *Ibid.*, p. 14. Asked about the adequacy of their income, 70 percent of the respondents said they had enough money to meet their monthly expenses.

5. *Ibid.*, p. 24.

6. Diep Trinh [personal interview], September 4, 2007.

7. Statistics Canada, "Selected Ethnic Origins for Census Metropolitan Areas and Census Agglomerations." The total comprises all those reporting Vietnamese, Cambodian or Laotian origins.

8. Statistics Canada, "Selected Cultural and Labour Force Characteristics." Because the data were presented by ethnic group, those identified as "Canadian" were taken as surrogates for the wider regional population. The rationale was twofold: the "Canadian" ethnic group was the largest; additionally, those who listed their ethnicity as "Canadian" might reasonably be supposed to feel well integrated into mainstream Canadian society. It should also be noted that averages for Southeast Asians as a group often mask significant differences among the core ethnic communities: Vietnamese, Cambodian and Laotian.

9. Statistics Canada, "Selected Income Characteristics."

10. Statistics Canada, "Selected Educational Characteristics." In most other categories, however, attained educational levels of the "Canadian" population remained higher than equivalent levels among the Southeast Asian communities.

11. Calculated from "Selected Educational Characteristics."

12. Huong Nguyen, "Reminiscences of a Former Refugee," *Vietnamese Bulletin*, Vol. 20., no. 4, pp.2-3. (October–December 2004).

13. Marion Dewar, as quoted in the *Vietnamese Bulletin*, *op. cit*.pp.8-9.

14. Vietnamese-Canadian Centre, *Survey of Socio-Economic Integration of Vietnamese Canadians*. Survey data specific to Ottawa were supplied by Can Le [personal communication], November 3, 2007.

BIBLIOGRAPHY

Books, Theses, Web Sites and Other Secondary Sources

_____1980. "Refugees: The Cry of the Indochinese" Tokyo: Asian Relations Center

Adelman, Howard. 1982 *Canada and the Indochinese Refugees*. Regina: L.A. Weigl Ltd.

Adelman, Howard (ed.). 1980. *The Indochinese Refugee Movement: The Canadian Experience*. Toronto: Operation Lifeline

Arndt, Joyce. 1983. The Private Sponsorship of the Indochinese Refugees [MA thesis, microform]. Ottawa: National Library of Canada

Beiser, Morton. 1999. *Strangers at the Gate: The "Boat People's" first ten years in Canada*. Toronto: University of Toronto Press

Canadian Broadcasting Corporation. "Pirates and Sinking Ships: One Refugee's Story" [radio broadcast]. July 29, 1979 [online]. Accessed February 28, 2007. http://archives.cbc.ca/.

Canadian Broadcasting Corporation. "Re-education Camps…or Death Camps?" [radio broadcast]. July 1, 1979 [online]. Accessed February 28, 2007. http://archives.cbc.ca/.

Canadian Broadcasting Corporation. "Refuge for the Unwanted" [television broadcast]. September 11, 1979 [online]. Accessed February 28, 2007. http://archives.cbc.ca/.

Canadian Museum of Civilization. Boat People No Longer [online]. A special year-long exhibition recounting the refugees' plight and the Canadian response. Hull (now Gatineau), Quebec: Canadian Museum of Civilization, 1998–99. Accessed February 26, 2007. www.civilization.ca and epe.lac-bac.gc.ca.

Chan, K.B., L.J. Dorais and D.M. Indra. 1988. *Ten Years Later: Indochinese Communities in Canada*. Montréal: Canadian Asian Studies Association

Dorais, L.J. 2000. *Les Cambodgiens, Laotiens, et Vietnamiens au Canada*. Ottawa: Société Historique du Canada

Duong, Lloyd. 2000. *The Boat People: Imprints on History*. Toronto: Optimal World Publishers

Employment and Immigration Canada. *Indochinese Refugees: The Canadian Response, 1979 and 1980*. Ottawa: Employment and Immigration Canada, 1982.

Fine-Meyer, Rose. 2003. "Unique Refugees: The Sponsorship and Resettlement of Vietnamese "Boat People" in Ontario, 1978–1980" [MA thesis, microform]. Ottawa: National Library of Canada

Grant, Bruce. 1979. *The Boat People: An Age Investigation*. Melbourne: Penguin Books

Harp, J. 1981. "Transformation of a social movement organization: The case of Project 4,000" Montréal: Institute for Research on Public Policy

Lam, Lawrence. 1996. *From Being Uprooted to Surviving: Resettlement of Vietnamese-Chinese "Boat People" in Montréal, 1980–1990*. Toronto: York Lane Press

Lavigne, Gabrielle, 2003. "Indochinese Refugees, Ste. Therese, Quebec, 1979–1982: Twenty Years Later" [MA thesis, microform]. Ottawa: National Library of Canada

Molloy, M. 1981. "The Indochinese Refugee Task Force, 1979–80." *C.I.H.S. Bulletin*. Vol. 51 (1981), pp. 1–3.

Nguyen, Huong. "Reminiscences of a Former Refugee." *Vietnamese Bulletin*. Vol. 20, no. 4. (October–December 2004).

Nguyen, S.D., T. Cooke and T.Q. Phung. *1983. Ottawa-Carleton Southeast Asian Refugees' Needs Assessment*. Ottawa: Ottawa-Carleton South-East Asian Refugee Project [Ottawa Room, Ottawa Public Library]

Pappone, R. 1982. *The* Hai Hong: *Profit, Tears and Joy*. Ottawa: Employment and Immigration Canada

Robinson, W.C. 1998. *Terms of Refuge*. London: Zed Books, 1998.

Rummel, R.J. 1997 Chapter 4, "Statistics of Cambodian Democide," and Chapter 6, "Statistics of Vietnamese Democide." In *Statistics of Democide: Genocide and Mass Murder Since 1900* [online]. Accessed May 15, 2007. www.hawaii.edu/powerkills.

Statistics Canada, "Selected Cultural and Labour Force Characteristics," *2001 Census* [online]. Catalogue number 97F0010XCB2001042. Accessed October 23, 2007. www.statcan12.ca.

Statistics Canada, "Selected Educational Characteristics," *2001 Census* [online]. Catalogue number 97F0010XCB 2001041. Accessed October 22, 2007. www.statcan12.ca.

Statistics Canada, "Selected Ethnic Origins for Census Metropolitan Areas and Census Agglomerations," *2001 Census* [online]. Accessed February 28, 2007. www.statcan12.ca.

Statistics Canada, "Selected Income Characteristics," *2001 Census* [online]. Catalogue number 97F0010XCB2001043. Accessed October 23, 2007. www.statcan12.ca.

Tepper, E.L. (ed.). 1980. *Southeast Asian Exodus: From Tradition to Resettlement*. Ottawa: Canadian Asian Studies Association.

United Nations High Commissioner for Refugees. 2000. Chapter 4, "Flight from Indochina." In *The State of the World's Refugees—2000* [online]. Accessed March 24, 2007. www.reliefweb.net/library/documents.

Other Web Sites Consulted

In addition to the sites specifically identified above, the following also proved useful, in terms of contents or links provided.

www.multiculturalcanada.ca. Accessed August 23, 2007.

web.ebscohost.com. Accessed May 15, 2007.

www.canadianencyclopedia.ca. Accessed March 21, 2007.

www.archives.cbc.ca. Accessed various dates, March–April 2007.

www.en.wikipedia.org. Accessed various dates, February–March 2007.

Interviews, Articles, Project 4000 Records and Other Primary Sources

Thirty-seven people generously shared their recollections with me; 33 in personal interviews carried out between May and November 2007, and the remainder by telephone and e-mail. In alphabetical order, the contributors were:

    Robert and Marilyn Bailey
    Stephen Blizzard
    Alan Breakspear
    Marion Dewar
    Liem Duong
    Tony Enns
    Barb and Dan Gamble
    Don Gerber
    Ian Hamilton
    Phyllis Hardie
    Richard Hardy
    An Song Hoang
    Rita Hughes
    Minh Huynh
    Bounkeo and Keo Khamphoune
    Chamroeun Lay
    Can Le
    Flora MacDonald
    Pat Marshall
    Russ Mills
    Mike Molloy
    Phuong Nguyen
    J. A. Plourde
    Sue and George Pike
    Elizabeth Rapley
    Huot Tea
    Elliot Tepper
    Ngoc Tran
    Diep Trinh
    Nancy and Doug Umbach
    Katherine Van Nguyen
    Peter Wiebe

Newspaper Articles

CP. "Canada to take more refugees", *Globe & Mail*, June 20, 1979.

Kinsman, P. "'Boat People' capture hearts of Ottawans", *Ottawa Citizen*, June 30, 1979, p.3

Maione, R. "Keep caring", *Ottawa Citizen*, [Letters] February 19, 1983.

McIntyre, A. "City rallies to refugee aid", *Ottawa Journal*, July 13, 1979, p.1.

Mills, R. "Helping you to help others", *Ottawa Citizen*, July 7, 1979.

Private Holdings

The most valuable written primary materials on Project 4000 were the documents conserved by Eleanor Ryan (referenced in the notes as the "Eleanor Ryan papers"). I owe her a particular debt of gratitude, as she provided access to a wealth of relevant papers, notably the minutes of the meetings of the board of directors, executive committee and joint management team/executive committee sessions, as well as correspondence, internal reports and the letters patent. In addition, her extensive set of newspaper clippings and back issues of the Project 4000 *Newsletter* were extremely helpful. The clippings conserved by Can Le, and a third set compiled independently by Elizabeth Rapley and Richard Hardy, offered valuable supplementary information. Selected materials supplied by the Vietnamese Canadian Federation, notably copies of the *Vietnamese Bulletin* and internal survey results, were also very useful.

Municipal Archives

The Archives of the City of Ottawa possess an extensive collection of original documents pertaining the Project 4000. I reviewed the following in preparing this work:

RG 7-11-3, Papers of Mayor Marion Dewar – Project 4000, Box 91.

Project 4000 Papers, boxes A8/3d, A8/4c, A8/5a, A8/5b, A8/5c, A8/5d, A8/6a.

Minutes of City Council meetings, selected sessions.

Unpublished Reports

Clarke, A. 1980. Final Report to the Board of Directors [Eleanor Ryan papers].

Marshall, P. and B. Bergin. 2003. The Early History of OCISO.

Rapley, E. 1997. The Archdiocese's Involvement with Immigrants: Fifty Years of Growth.

Vietnamese Canadian Centre. *Survey of Socio-Economic Integration of Vietnamese Canadians*. Ottawa: Vietnamese Canadian Centre, 2004–2005.

INDEX

INDEX OF PERSONS AND PLACES

Asia and the Pacific, 6, 11
Aylmer, 57
Australia, 1, 11, 24, 26
Bailey, Marilyn, 51
Bailey, Robert, 51
Blizzard, Stephen, 18
Breakspear, Alan, 34, 36, 42, 44
Cambodia, 1, 5, 7, 9, 11, 20-21, 52, 56, 68-69, 72
Canada, 2-3, 16-18, 21, 27, 29, 31-33, 39, 48, 53, 57, 65, 67-69, 71-76, 79, 83
Centretown, viii
China, 6, 10
Chinatown, 49
Clark, Joe, 1, 29, 45, 53, 71
Clarke, Alan, 59
City Hall, see Ottawa
Cockburn, Bruce, 37
Cumberland, 62
Dewar, Ken, 30-31
Dewar, Marion, 2, 30-34, 36-38, 40, 42, 45, 51, 53, 61, 70-72, 81
Dien Bien Phu, 6
Duong, Liem, 56-57
Enns, Tony, 52
France, 5
Gamble, Barb, 37, 45, 60
Gamble, Dan, 37, 44-45
Geneva, 2, 6, 26

Gerber, Don, 39, 41
Hamilton, Ian, 16-17, 24
Hanoi, 6-7, 10
Hanover, 57
Hardie, Phyllis, 57, 61
Hardy, Richard, 33
Hoang, An Song, viii, 61-62, 83-85
Ho Chi Minh, 5
Ho Chi Minh City, 8
Hong Kong, 11-12, 19, 24
Hughes, Rita, 62-63
Huynh, Minh, 65
Indonesia, 11, 26
Japan, 5
Kampuchea, see Cambodia
Khamphoune, Bounkeo, 65
Khamphoune, Keo, 65
Lansdowne Park, 32-33, 36-41, 44
Laos, 1, 5, 10-11, 20-21, 52, 56, 65, 72
Lay, Chamroeun, 48-49, 69-70
Le, Can, 31, 53, 62
Le, Vuong, 53
Lubbock, Michael, 34, 42
Luu Family, 17
MacDonald, Flora, 1-3, 26, 29, 71
Maione, Romeo, 60-61
Malaysia, 11, 14, 19, 26
Marshall, Pat, 52, 69

Mills, Russ, 33, 35
Molloy, Mike, 71
Montréal, 68, 76
Nansen Medal, 2, 27
Nguyen, Huong, 79-80
Nguyen, Phuong, 62-63, 67, 69
Nixon, Richard, see United States of America
North America, 1, 26, 74
North Bay, 18
North Korea, 6
North Vietnam, see Vietnam
Ontario, 57, 73
Ottawa, viii, 2-3, 30-36, 41-42, 45, 48, 51, 55-56, 60-62, 65, 68, 70-73, 76, 81
Paris, 6-7
Philippines, 11, 26
Pike, George, 37-38, 47-48, 69
Pike, Sue, 37-38, 47, 69
Plourde, J-A, 39, 68, 70
Pol Pot, 7, 9-10
Port Klang, 15
Preah Vihear, 19
Québec, 68, 73
Rapley, Elizabeth, 55
Rideau Canal, 57
Rideau Hall, 64
Robinson, William, 39
Ryan, Eleanor, 64
Saigon, 6-9, 20

Sartre, Jean-Paul, 25
Singapore, 11-12, 14, 19, 26
South China Sea, viii, 21-22, 61
Southeast Asia, 7, 16, 25, 37, 59, 74
South Korea, 6, 11
South Vietnam, see Vietnam
Soviet Union, 6
Spratly Islands, 24
Tea, Huot, 68
Tepper, Elliot, 71
Thailand, 10-11, 14, 21-22, 26, 61
Tokyo, 2, 29
Toronto, 68, 71, 76
Trinh, Diep, 53-55, 63, 66-67
Trinh, Tam, 53-55, 63
Umbach, Doug, 57
Umbach, Nancy, 57
United Nations High Commissioner for Refugees (UNHCR), 2, 18-19, 26-27
United States of America, 6-8
Van Nguyen, Katherine, 68
Vancouver, 70, 76
Vietnam, viii, 1, 5-8, 10, 12, 15, 20, 23, 25-26, 52, 56, 61-62, 72, 79, 81
Washington, see United States of America
Western Europe, 1, 26
Wiebe, Peter, 69

ABOUT THE AUTHOR

BRIAN BUCKLEY

Brian Buckley was born in Montréal and educated in Montréal and Ottawa. He joined Canada's career foreign service in 1967 and retired in 1998 with the rank of Director General after postings in the Middle East, Europe, and the United States. After three years at Dalhousie University in Halifax he returned to Ottawa and began lecturing at Carleton University's Norman Paterson School of International Affairs. He is the author of several books and journal articles on foreign affairs and the news media, and Canada's early nuclear programs. He and his wife Mary Ann have five children and a growing number of grandchildren. In 1979-80 Brian and Mary Ann participated in Project 4000 as members of a sponsorship group in Ottawa's Alta Vista area.

To order more copies of

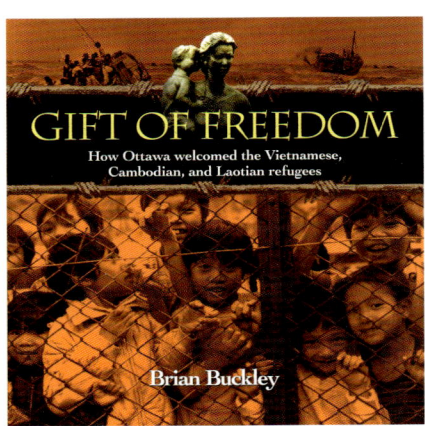

Contact:
**GENERAL STORE
PUBLISHING HOUSE**

499 O'Brien Road, Box 415
Renfrew, Ontario Canada K7V 4A6
Telephone: 1-800-465-6072
Fax: (613) 432-7184
www.gsph.com

VISA and MASTERCARD accepted.